Carpe Audience

Give Better Presentations Despite PowerPoint

John-Michael Keyes

Carpe Audience
Give Better Presentations Despite PowerPoint

John-Michael Keyes

ISBN-13: 978-1460980316
ISBN-10: 146098031X

GRAPHIC DESIGN

This book was designed by The Keyes Firm, LLC using Adobe Illustrator®, Adobe Photoshop® and Pages on Apple Macintosh® computers.

The Keyes Firm, LLC
P.O. Box 551
Bailey, CO 80421

TRADEMARK INFORMATION

Apple, Keynote, Microsoft, and PowerPoint are trademarks of their respective companies and may be registered in certain jurisdictions. Carpe Audience™ and Carpe Way™ are Trademarks of The Keyes Firm, LLC and may be registered in certain jurisdictions.

WARNING AND DISCLAIMER

This book is sold as is, without warranty of any kind, either express or implied. Techniques outlined in this book have been used successfully in front of live audiences with positive, measured results. Your mileage may vary. Good luck, and Carpe Audience.

Yesterday is gone.

Tomorrow has not yet come.

We have only today.

Let us begin.

Mother Teresa

CONTENTS

The caterpillar does all the work but the butterfly gets all the publicity.

George Carlin

Forward _____ **10**
In The Beginning
In The Middle
In The End

Introduction _____ **12**
The Ancient Art Of PowerPoint
Harnessing The Ancient Power Of Presentation
Ancient Power, Meet Nemesis
It's A Damn Shame
It Gets Even Worse
You Haven't Really Been Brainwashed. Not You
The Visceral Shift
You Ruined Me

Revealing The Secret Formulas _____ **16**
Learning And Using The Secret Formulas
Background
Here We Go
About This Book
Other Venues

You've Been Bamboozled _____ **20**
PowerPoint Is Not...
Your Slides Are Not A TelePrompter
Your Slides Are Not Your Presentation
Your Slides Are Not Your Handout
OK, I've Been Fooled, Now What?

Learn MultiMedia Learning _____ **24**
Cognitive Science And Multimedia Learning
Standing On The Shoulders Of Giants
Dual Channels – Pictorial And Verbal
The Catch
Words Are Tricky
Bad, Bad Cognitive Overload
Vision Wins
We Don't Pay Attention To Boring Things
Emotions Get Our Attention

Pictures. Lots Of Pictures
This Ain't Main Street. It's Hollywood
Audio, The Other Provocateur
The 10 Minute Barrier
Repeat To Remember

Who Are These People And Why Are They Here? _____30

Campfire Theory
You Have The Talking Stick
The Sweat Lodge
Audience Matters
Audience Conditioning
Remember 10 Minutes?
See It In Action
The First 10 Minutes (600 Seconds)
Next 2 Minutes
The Next 10 Minutes
The Last 8 Minutes
Leveraging The 30 Second Attention Span
Embrace And Extend
Visual Syncopation

Everything Is A Story. Everything _____38

Everything Is A Story. Everything
Say Nothing Without A Purpose
Starting From The End
The Pen Is Mightier Than The Mouse. Until It Isn't
Back To The End
Writing The Story
Sequencing
Create A Cadence Worksheet

Crayons And Napkins _____42

You Really Need To Do This
Bars And Talking Sticks
One More Thing
While The Crayons Are Still Hot
PowerPoint Rules Of Thumb And Other Things That Are Incredibly Stupid
The Stupid Rule Of Six
The Stupid Two Minute Rule
The Stupid 36 Point, Font Size Rule
Stupid, Stupid Clip Art
Stupid, Stupid, Stupid Bullet Points
More Stupid: Title All Of Your Slides With A Heading
The Words "In Summary" Mean "Oh, Thank God It's Over"

Guerilla Typography _____46

Guerilla Typography
Consistency Is Critical
The Guerilla Recipe
Font Types
Font Weight
Font Measurements
Kerning

Tracking
Leading
Applied Knowledge
To Cap Or Not To Cap
Finding Free Fonts
Spell Check

Signal To Noise Ratio _____ **56**
Unsucking Your Templates
Signal To Noise Ratio
Backgrounds
Black. Like The Night. Where Campfires Live
Back To Templates - Your Logo
Aspect Ratio
Template Designs - Three Or Four Or Five Or Six
Black And White
Master Templates
Format Text Effects
Paragraph
Slide Transitions

Technique D'Slide _____ **62**
The Very First Slide
Deconstruction
The Power List: "Kill The Bullets"
The Power List: "Common Elements"
The Power List: "Isolated Info"
The Power List: "Highlight The Fact"

Image Surfing _____ **68**
Pictures
Free Association Image Surfing Technique
No More Than Three Minutes.
Copyrights, Usage And Shyness

The Grid _____ **70**
So Simple It Must Be A Trick

Trick Photography _____ **74**
Photography Tricks
No Montages. No! None
Crop Or Bleed
Resolution
Adding Type
Anamorphic Scaling

Charts And Graphs _____ **78**
Graphs Are The Last Resort. Unless They're The First
Finding The Point
TMI - Detail Is For The Report Or Handout
Chartoholics Shout Disapproval

Using Multimedia _____ **82**
How Cool Is That?
Collateral Damage In The Battles Of Giants

The Internet Will Not Exist At Your Next Gig
YouTube Ripping And Hoisting The Jolly Roger
The Mashable List
Web Based
Windows Applications
Linux
OS X
Plugins

Slide Herding _____ 88
Let's Saddle Up PowerPoint (Or Keynote)
Put A Sticky Note On Your Monitor
Collect Your Stories
Adding Presenter Notes
Stick With Your Templates
Look At Your Napkins
Look For Visual Syncopation Opportunities
Verify Registration Between Slides
Transitions Between Slides
Animation On The Slide
Sexy Animated Curvy Arrows
Internet Dependency
It's Time To March

Essential Is Rehearsal _____ 92
Practice Makes Perfect
Stand Up. Speak Out
Use Your Clicker
It's Rehearsal Not Memorization
First Pass
Try, Try Again
Add 10%

Master The Presenter View And Rule The World _____ 94
What You See Is What You Get. Or Not
The Catch

Lights Camera Campfire _____ 96
The Gifts
Butterflies? You're A Rock Star
Swagger? You're Not Really A Rock Star
Swaggering Butterflies
David Grossman And Deep Breaths
Scouting
Clothes
Pockets
Lecterns And Podiums
Lavaliere Microphones
Lights
Learn Silence
Learn To Shout
Learn To Whisper
Jokes Are For Comedians
Where Humor Works

Turn Off Sleep Mode, Display Sleep And Hibernation
Count Your Blessings Then Use Them
Inventory Your Curses And Overcome Them
Carpe Audience

Lights Camera Sweat Lodge _____102
The Boardroom
The Update
The Pitch
Hyperlinking Is The Answer. What's The Question?
Make It So
Work It Baby. Work It

Handout Theory _____106
When You Go To A Movie, Do You Bring The Script?
Why Not Ask What They Do With Their Handouts?
The Other Handout

Gear _____114
Presentation Gear And Stuff
Get A Clicker Immediately. Go! Now!
Testing, One, Two, Three
Be A TV Star
Adapters And Cables
Batteries
Gaffer's Or Duct Tape
If You're Really Serious, Get A Projector
Your Studio. Yes, I Called Your Office A Studio
My Studio

Ravings _____118
A Short Rant On The PowerPoint User Interface
Anymore, It's Keynote

Photo Credits _____120
Where'd You Get All This Stuff_____124
References

HOW
DID I
NOT
KNOW
THIS

> **"** Every closed eye is not sleeping, and every open eye is not seeing. **"**
>
> *Bill Cosby*

IN THE BEGINNING

I was there when the first proto-Carpe presentation was made. As an invited guest of John-Michael Keyes for what was to be the introduction of a program later dubbed the National School Safety Collaborative, I knew to expect something great, but had no idea that I would experience something so different, so right, and so elementally attention grabbing. In the intervening couple of years, I've watched as his Carpe Audience technique improved incrementally. I encountered each new presentation with growing astonishment and envy. Carpe Audience is one of those elementally true things…those things that you know are the answer to a problem you didn't quite know you had, but you recognize as soon as a solution is proposed. It's a mind shift, for certain. It's also work, but such worthwhile labor! In the same way that watching the preparation of a great meal is a multi-sensory experience, watching a Carpe Audience presentation is a full and imminently satisfying journey.

IN THE MIDDLE

I've also had the heady rush of bringing a Carpe presentation to life. I reluctantly signed on as an early beta tester, and created a new presentation for an audience that was very important to me. The experience was amazing! A funny thing happens when you start to think in terms of storytelling, and making points in a way that will be memorable. You begin to scan your world for poignant images. You see symbolism in simple exchanges. You wake up with an image in your head that **must** be added to your slide set. And you watch other people present regrettable bulleted lists and wonder how much more their presentation would have meant if they had been cognizant of the Carpe Way. It's true that I worried and whined through the process of developing my first Carpe presentation…and then it was a success. I was glad about that, but even more profoundly moved that it had felt to me like the right thing to do. These methods connect you to your audience differently, and it's a really good thing.

IN THE END

Incorporating any of these tips is likely to increase the energy of your next presentation. I will bet you that those moments will stand out for you. And I'll wager that you'll be back. The tricks and techniques in this book sometimes feel like deception. Let's be fair, when we do a post hoc evaluation of this year's great Super Bowl commercials, we know we've been subjected to marketing and entertainment tricks. Does that make our enjoyment of the ads any less? I don't think so. In fact, we watch for those great ads and expect them each year. Will Carpe Audience make us equally spoiled, expecting an excellent presentation at nearly every turn? Maybe. Possibly. Probably! My hope is that we'll become more demanding of our speakers. Is this a problem? Is using Carpe Audience an unfair advantage? My only answer is, if we have to sit through the presentation, oughtn't it be engaging?

John-Michael Keyes believes in the method he has detailed in this book. He emphasizes that, in a presentation, it is the speaker who has been given the gift of our time and attention. Mr. Keyes insists that the speaker repay that gift with a gift of equal worth. Carpe Audience.

Lee Shaughnessy

There have been
great societies that
did not use the
wheel, but there
have been no
societies that
did not tell stories.

Ursula K. LeGuin

THE ANCIENT ART OF POWERPOINT

It's become a synonym. PowerPoint equals Presentation. If you think about it, it's the oldest, most powerful, mass communication strategy humans have ever deployed. Part storytelling, part performance, part props and part pictures, presenting to an audience is an ancient art. If you believe the synonym, then the first version of PowerPoint was developed by our ancestors when they were still living in caves. Maybe a stick scratching the cave floor as an elder explained "Spear Theory Revealed" to a handful of the tribe's wide-eyed youth.

" Even **stick figures**, drawn on the cave floor, enhanced communication in humans."

The stick and the props were the secret. In addition to the verbal information, visual support was added. Through demonstration and through pictures. Even stick figures, drawn on the cave floor, enhanced the communication and the learning process in humans. Dramatically.

From the cave floor, to the cave wall, to the blackboard to the flip chart, to the projector, the art of PowerPoint (syn. presentation) has been used in one form or another by every culture on the planet.

HARNESSING THE ANCIENT POWER OF PRESENTATION

If you would have asked me two years ago, "What's an outreach campaign?" I couldn't have produced a credible answer. But I learned. I learned the Ancient Power of Presentation. How going into a room and "Presenting" a concept, telling stories, calling for action from the audience, and having support materials easily accessible, could ignite a movement. Might even change the world. I also learned that people are hungry for great presentations and I got invited to more. Many more. In the course of under two years, I gave nearly a hundred presentations in 12 states and over 40 cities. Ballrooms. Boardrooms. Conference rooms. Classrooms. Auditoriums. High School Gyms.

In less than two years, that concept, "The Standard Response Protocol,[1]" has been adopted in nearly two thousand schools across the country. Over a million kids, teachers, cops and fire fighters are being trained (with a PowerPoint Presentation) in the protocol. Less than two years. Just by "Presenting."

ANCIENT POWER, MEET NEMESIS

For thousands of years the Ancient Power of Presentation has survived the rise and fall of civilizations and the onslaught of technology. Even moveable type and the cotton gin. Until now. The Ancient Power of Presentation has been weakened by a dark nemesis... Microsoft.

Now Microsoft wasn't the first company, nor the last, to create presentation software. But the combination of Microsoft's corporate culture, monopoly, feature-seek, marketing and misguided development priorities resulted in the PowerPoint juggernaut that has redefined what a "Presentation" should be.

IT'S A DAMN SHAME

And that's a damn shame. Because the core elements to create a truly great presentation exist within the framework of the application we call PowerPoint. But they're hidden, or hard to use, or ignored. Instead PowerPoint, the application, manifested as a tool designed by software engineers, not presenters, to deliver detailed information, initially to other software engineers.

If you've met many software engineers, then you probably already know that they're typically not very good storytellers. Not very good presenters. They are very good at putting large data structures in their heads. At thinking in booleans and switches and subroutines. They are the stereotypical smart-kid geeks you remember from high school.

Here's what happened. As the computer revolution brought machines to our desktops, complexity and learning curves turned many of us into intellectual toddlers. We trusted the smart people, the people who knew how these crazy computer things worked, to be experts. And they were. At working computers.

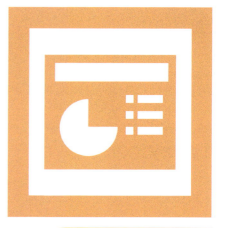

> " They slid their methods, their ethos and their **engineering parts lists,** into the default..."

When we blindly extended the perception of their expertise to other areas, they slid their methods, their ethos, their engineering parts lists, into the default behavior of PowerPoint. In less than a generation it became the "PowerPoint Way." Suddenly, because Microsoft said it should be that way, it was. Heck.

IT GETS EVEN WORSE

The Microsoft domination couldn't be ignored and a whole economy sprang up to support this new paradigm of what a presentation should look like. Documents and services sprouted from vendors around the planet that mirrored the new structure that was the default PowerPoint template. Competitors had to include compatibility and similar features and interfaces.

It doesn't matter what version, what generation, the bullet list is in the very core identity of PowerPoint.

It left us, mere mortals, in the face of this growing, glowing deity, brainwashed into believing, "Verily, this is so."

YOU HAVEN'T REALLY BEEN BRAINWASHED. NOT YOU

This book is about regaining your cultural roots. About tapping into the most powerful communication method known to mankind. About relearning the Ancient Power of Presentation. It's about an intervention and rescuing you from the cult of Microsoft. And I use science to do it. Not some fuzzy anecdotes or feelings. Cold, hard, clinical science.

A data analyst said about some of the techniques described in this book. "That artsy stuff might be fine for CEOs and keynote speeches, but if I did that I'd be laughed out the company door."

Great stories teach you something. That's one reason I haven't slipped into some sort of retirement. I always feel like I'm learning something new.

Clint Eastwood

I have a couple of simple questions. Why do you think they are CEOs? Why is it the CEO is getting to keynote? Why do you think your co-workers aren't already laughing, or worse, crying about your current presentation method? Oh yeah, tell me again exactly how long you've been a data analyst?

The stuff in this book works. It will make you a better presenter. Like anything new though, it will take work. You might stub your toe when you're on the path to greatness. Doesn't mean you should turn around on the path. Keep limping forward until the sting is gone.

It works in boardrooms and in classrooms and in conference rooms. Educators, you especially should pay attention to the techniques and practices described in this book. You are a MSCBT® (Microsoft Certified Brainwashing Technician). If you introduce kids from kindergarten on up, to the cult of Microsoft they too will begin to believe mediocre or even bad is only way.

THE VISCERAL SHIFT

Here's where it gets interesling. Even if you take baby steps and just try a couple of these techniques, you will most likely experience more successful presentation outcomes. Just like your audience is hungry for great presentations, you will begin to feel the appetite for giving great presentations. The hunger to seize the crowd, and engage.

You will come back to this book for more.

At some point you will become fluent in the Carpe Way. You won't think in bullet lists. You'll think in terms of "call to action," and single images and stories and words and rehearsal. You'll find that presentations begin to write themselves once you have a story in mind, and you won't need crayons and napkins.

YOU RUINED ME

It may also ruin you. I got a call from one of the early reviewers of this book. She helped with some edits and structure and concepts in this book. She began to build her next presentation in the Carpe Way. And she said, "You ruined me."

"Pardon?"

"You ruined me, I can't *look* at a conventional PowerPoint anymore without cringing inside. It's horrible how bad they are."

" We strayed from the Ancient Power, but we **can** come back."

Yes. They are. We strayed from the Ancient Power, but we can come back. We can learn from both our ancestors and the lab. We can override the defaults and we can open our eyes. We can even change the world, one presentation at a time.

Carpe Audience.

REVEALING
THE SECRET
FORMULAS

> **"**
> Words are,
> of course,
> the most
> powerful drug
> used by mankind.
> **"**
>
> *Rudyard Kipling*

LEARNING AND USING THE SECRET FORMULAS

At some point in time, almost every professional experiences it... The boss walks in and says, "Can you put together a PowerPoint for blah, blah, blah." After the initial "Evil Boss" thought, the professional thinks to him or herself, "I have to do a PowerPoint presentation? In front of other humans? All alone?" For many, dread clenches their souls in a black-gloved fist.

Let's take a moment and deconstruct that scenario. The first challenge is that the evil boss put the cart before the horse. She asked you to do a PowerPoint, not give a presentation. If pressed though, she would ultimately realize that she wants you to give a presentation and use Power-Point (or Keynote) to support your presentation.

The other point of heartburn is all yours. You see, the thought that you *have* to give a presentation is really wrong-headed. Turn it around and think, "I *get* to do a presentation."

Here's the deal. Whether it's occasionally or frequently, you can give bel-ter presentations. Really. It just takes a shift in perspective. And breaking some bad habits. And learning from some unexpected sources. There are also some formulas that you can apply to your presentation and de-livery that will increase your ability to provide your message to your audi-ence effectively.

Just as important is the science. There has been a great deal of work in the areas of cognitive science and multimedia learning. This research has a direct bearing on how to design and deliver great presentations.

Release my inner child?
I only have a **tenuous grasp** on my
outer adult.**"**

There is also some kid stuff. For instance, crayons. And napkins. Seri-ously, one technique for creating your presentation visuals is to forget PowerPoint and instead build your entire slide show, one napkin at a time, using crayons. Have at it. Release your inner child. Damn bullet lists just don't fit do they? When you're done with your napkins, and the crayons are put neatly away, then fire up PowerPoint.

BACKGROUND

Over my career I've given presentations. Sales presentations. Progress or project presentations. Product demonstrations. Sometimes, presenta-tions from the heart. I wasn't terribly bad at delivering presentations. But, not necessarily great either.

In 2006, I started delivering webinars. A few a week. Sales or technical mini-presentations without the benefit of eye-contact or the silent lan-guage of face to face interaction. What was cool though, was the ability to record the meeting for debriefing later. While reviewing these I discov-ered a cadence, a deliberate timing that made the presentation more effective. And this cadence is predictable and repeatable.

2006 also brought tragedy into my family. Under any circumstance the death of a child is difficult. Although, from my personal perspective, it does seem magnified when the event becomes a national media story. One of our family responses was to create The "I Love U Guys" Foundation.[2]

In January of 2009, I shifted my professional experience to work entirely on the efforts of the foundation. It really felt like a John Sculley[3] moment, "Do I want to write and peddle software for bankers, lawyers and collectors or can I change the world?" I chose the latter. It turns out that changing the world, in this case, involved developing and delivering presentations.

HERE WE GO

My first presentation for the foundation was in my living room in April of 2009. Friends and family. A safe harbor to practice with people. A week later was a firehouse in Bailey, Colorado. By June I was giving lots of presentations. Plenaries, keynotes, workshops or just meetings with a couple of folks around a table. Not just local audiences either. Within a few months I was keynoting at national conferences. An outcome that rests firmly on presentation quality. Not necessarily the presenter. Some of these were video taped, so I could later see what the crowd saw.

But before I delivered that first living room presentation, I committed to understanding how to give the best possible presentation I could. I began doing some cursory research. I started with a little e-book by Seth Godin[4] about how to avoid bad PowerPoint. I danced a little with Richard Mayer's[5] work on multimedia learning (although later I dug much deeper). Garr Reynolds'[6] material was another influential source of information. (Although for the longest time, I relied solely on online availability.)

With a frequency of about one presentation a week, and a commitment to giving the best presentation possible, I ended up attending conferences. It gave me an opportunity to see more presentations. (A lot more presentations.) So I watched. What worked. What didn't.

" Nearly **80%** of the presenters read **bullet lists** from screen."

Almost every presenter had a PowerPoint. Almost every PowerPoint was at best gruesome. Nearly 80% of the presenters read all or part of their presentation from barely discernible bullet lists. But, there were some, that despite the horrid slides, were still pretty good presentations. What was interesting was that presenters with good slides gave pretty good presentations. My thought on that is this: If you are committed to giving a good presentation, then you know that bad slides don't help.

While bad slides don't necessarily kill your presentation, they can certainly diminish its impact. Or diminish your credibility. Or they will indeed kill your presentation. I have seen bad PowerPoint distract even the presenter with its horridness.

From my living room to the conference room to the training room to the ballroom to the auditorium. What a ride.

This is a from Legend High School in Parker, Colorado. Big stage. Big screen. Big sound. I love high school auditoriums. Especially when the theater director is a gear head. (I heart sub-woofers.)

You can wreck a communication process with lousy logic or unsupported facts, but you can't complete it without emotion.

Logic is not enough.

Seth Godin

Perhaps a metaphor… If your presentation was a newspaper, then each slide is a headline and you are the story.

ABOUT THIS BOOK

This book isn't about public speaking. There are at least a jillion books on that topic. But if you're building your very first presentation or you're looking at amping up some of your current work, this book should be worth the read. If you need a little brush up on public speaking, one of my favorites is **Presentation Training A-Z**[7] by T.J. Walker. Here's a revelation. I didn't discover T.J. until this book was already mostly written. Guarantee you, I wish I would have sooner. What's weird is I don't know how I missed him, cuz I did a ton of research. Lots. Stayed up late.

Keep in mind, this book isn't a how-to manual on "PowerPoint" the software (although, there may be some useful gems that took me forever to find), rather a collection of observations, theories, science, declarations and occasional rants on how to design and create a better presentation. How to keep PowerPoint from interfering with your presentation. How to make PowerPoint give your presentations more impact.

" This stuff takes **work**."

The other thing to keep in mind with this book is that creating and executing great presentations takes work. If you want a simple-answer, silver-bullet, just-do-this, guide to excellent presentation creation and delivery, this isn't the book for you.

There may be some "Naturals" out there. But I haven't found them. Most of the great presentations that make the presenter look like a "Natural," were the result of hard work on the part of the presenter. These presenters wrote and tweaked and tuned their presentations. And they practiced. Not a little. A lot. They used airplane time to work it. They practiced after dinner. They asked family, friends and colleagues to not only watch dress rehearsals, but give feedback. They listened. Sometimes, they incorporated suggested changes. Sometimes they didn't.

They also watch other presenters. Ingraining the "craft" of presenting. They often video tape themselves and review the tapes. Delivering a great presentation takes elbow grease in advance. And a thick skin in order to understand and remedy points of criticism.

OTHER VENUES

Webinars, keynotes, workshops, plenaries. Of these I can speak. I've had success with executive presentations, classrooms and meetings. Courtrooms, sermons or other venues? Well, I suspect the advice in this book applies. But, your mileage may vary.

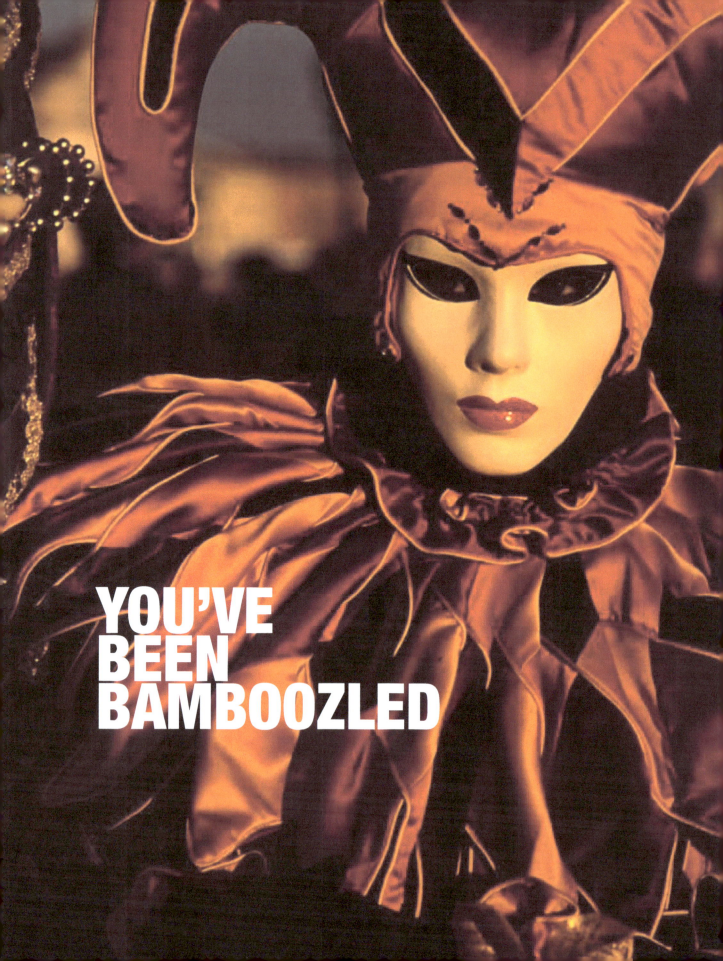

> **"**
> It was
> beautiful
> and simple,
> as all
> truly great
> swindles
> are...
> **"**
>
> *O'Henry*

POWERPOINT IS NOT...

Repeat after me: PowerPoint is not a teleprompter. PowerPoint is not your presentation. PowerPoint is not your handout. Not.

YOUR SLIDES ARE NOT A TELEPROMPTER

You've been bamboozled. The problem with most presentations is that people are taught PowerPoint skills. Not presentation skills. And Power-Point has fatal flaws when looked at in the context of enhanced learning. The default state of PowerPoint (or even Keynote for that matter) is the channeling of text into bullet lists. It bears repeating: The default state of PowerPoint is to channel text into bullet lists, not to help you visually enhance learning.

Often those bullet lists are projected on a screen as a presenter reads the list. I call this presentation strategy "consensual teleprompting." There is even a Karaoke version of this technique which involves using a laser pointer and targeting each word on screen as the presenter reads it.

" consensual teleprompting
ultimately **leads to sleep...**
without the afterglow.**"**

Because we've seen consensual teleprompting some folks might believe it's an acceptable presentation method. Pshaw. You've been bamboo-zled. That is simply "Death by PowerPoint." Just because you've seen smart, articulate, expert people deliver presentations this way, doesn't mean it's the best way. If you explore cognitive theory (and we will later in this book) you'll discover that consensual teleprompting actually reduces learning and sharply decreases audience attention.

If you need a teleprompter, then your presenter notes are your tele-prompter. And those are carefully screened away from your audience. "Presenter View" is an option with PowerPoint and "Presenter Display" with Keynote. Either shows your notes on the laptop screen and the slides on the projector. See the "Master the Presenter View and Rule the World," chapter later in this book.

YOUR SLIDES ARE NOT YOUR PRESENTATION

The next bamboozlement is that someone seeing just your slides would be able to get your presentation. That isn't what slides are for. That's what brochures or books or reports or a video of you delivering your presentation are for. Understand the medium. PowerPoint is not a desk-top publishing program. You may have been fooled into thinking it might be, but it really is about presenting text or graphics in support of your delivery.

This bamboozlement is so widespread though, that some conferences ask for the slides in advance. They may even want to reformat them into some consistent (usually ugly) template. Resist that. Send them your handout (see "Handout Theory") and gently suggest that you have a multimedia experience that would be challenging to integrate into another template. Your slides are there to support your conversation with your audience. Not try to have it.

YOUR SLIDES ARE NOT YOUR HANDOUT

With one click of the mouse, PowerPoint lets you print thumbnails of your slides with lines next to it. And the clever jesters at Microsoft called this feature a "Handout." They may even believe it themselves. But miniature pictures of your slides are not a handout. That is the lazy way, not the Carpe Way. It's a waste of paper and diminishes the effectiveness of your presentation.

> **"** They **read ahead**, mentally adjust how much time is left as the presentation continues, and they'll write notes on maybe 4 of the **little lines**. **"**

Having your presentation in people's hands before they see it diminishes it. Surprise is not just a useful tool when delivering a presentation, you will see that it's an essential tool. And if folks have your entire slide deck in hand, in advance, they do exactly what you would do. They read ahead, mentally adjust how much time is left as the presentation continues, and they'll write notes on maybe 4 of the little lines. What you've given them with your handout is an easy way to not pay attention to you – the presenter. So think about it. When you want to give your audience every ability to pay attention to you, the first thing you do is hand them a distraction? Duh?

With all of that said, audiences have been bamboozled too. Often they want a handout. It's expected. There is a whole section on handout theory that answers the audience demand of having a handout without giving them a built in distraction.

OK, I'VE BEEN FOOLED, NOW WHAT?

The next section of this book is about the science behind human learning. I'll point to some hard science that supports the Carpe Audience presentation philosophy.

But first, the next page shows a slide show that I found at http://slideshare.net.[8] I am totally serious... This is a presentation about effective business communication. It's shown here for example purposes, but do take a moment and look at every slide and put it into the context of its purported purpose: A presentation on "Effective Business Communication," etc.

Effective business communications and barriers of communications

What is communication?

- The transfer and understanding of meaning.
- Effective communication is when a transmitted thought or idea is received and understood by the receiver as it was intended by the sender; it doesn't mean agreement with the transmitted thought or idea.
- Communication encompasses both INTERPERSONAL and ORGANIZATIONAL.

Basic principles of communication

- use open ended and close ended questions appropriately
- use eye contact, encouraging gestures
- focus on the situation, issue, behavior, not the person
- maintain the self-confidence and self-esteem of others
- maintain constructive relationships with your employees, peers, managers
- use active listening techniques such as stating your understanding of what you are hearing
- make sure you summarize
- lead by example

7 elements of communication process

(A message travel along)

Message — MEDIUM — RECIEVER

Encoding (converting a message into symbols)

Decoding (re-translating sender's message)

SENDER — NOISE — Message

FEEDBACK

(To check both side whether understood the message)

In order to facilitate effective communication, we must first understand how the process works. Information is conveyed as words, tone of voice, and body language. Studies have shown as follow:-

- 7% words of the information communicated.
- 38% vocal tone (verbal intonation/Paralinguistic))
- 55% of body language

Barriers of Communication

- **Filtering** – telling the receiver what he/she wants to hear
- **Emotional**- How a sender/ receiver feels when sending/interpreting a message
- **Information overload** – information we have to work exceed our processing capacity
- **Defensiveness** – When a person feels he/she is threatened
- **Cultural Barriers** – Differences in habits/ Cultures
- **Language** – choice of words or language in which a sender encodes a message
- **Gender barriers** - distinct differences between the speech patterns in a man and those in a woman

Effective communications skills

- Acknowledge ("Roger") communications.
- Provide information in accordance with SOP's.
- Provide information when asked.
- Repeat, as necessary, to ensure communication is accurately received.
- Use standard terminology when communicating information.
- Request and provide clarification when needed.
- Ensure statements are direct and unambiguous.
- Inform the appropriate individuals when the mission or plans change.
- Communicate all information needed by those individuals or teams external to the team.
- Use nonverbal communication appropriately.
- Use proper order when communicating information

Other barriers of communication

- Sender breakdown – too much information is being sent, so the recipient misses key points.
- Method breakdown – when information is very detailed or complicated, then written instructions are better than messages which can be misinterpreted.
- Recipient breakdown – the recipient deliberately makes a choice to misinterpret the message because of their attitude to either the sender to the message at hand.
- Long chain of command
- Vague purpose – message not detailed enough, m ore explanation required
- Inappropriate medium – eg, A manager uses short message service(sms) to his employee to get work done, when it should have been communicated verbally, so that instructions are clear.
- Red tape – message gets passed on to many different people before finally reaching the recipient, making the process too long and the message changing. Also, actions can be delayed as a result of a late arrival of the message.
- Status of 2 parties – can be intimidated by the other person's status because of their gender, age, etc
- Distraction – communication channels breaking up, for example, an insurance agent going through his client's portfolio in a crowded food centre. The client will not be able to concentrate on what he is trying to say and thus will not be in the right state of mind to do any investing.

LEARN
MULTIMEDIA
LEARNING

> The most dangerous strategy is to cross the chasm in two leaps.

Bob Jueneman

COGNITIVE SCIENCE AND MULTIMEDIA LEARNING

As we delve into presentation development, a look at the science behind how people learn is imperative. This is the part of PowerPoint training that is ignored in nearly every training or book. Making animated curvy arrows does not make a compelling and dynamic presentation. Really.

STANDING ON THE SHOULDERS OF GIANTS

In this section I draw heavily from the works of Mayer and Medina. The books referenced are:

Multimedia Learning[9], Richard Mayer
Brain Rules[10], John Medina

I'll be highlighting their conclusions. And, I might even be selective in what I regurgitate. If you are serious about presentations, then you might consider buying and reading the books.

In "Multimedia Learning," Richard Mayer conducted clinical experiments on the effectiveness of combining animation, text, graphics, images and narration. You know, like a PowerPoint presentation. The outcome of his research revealed that "people learn more deeply from words and pictures than from words alone."

DUAL CHANNELS – PICTORIAL AND VERBAL

The first assumption used in his research is that there are dual channels people use to process and retain information. Auditory/Verbal and Visual. It's important to highlight that the Auditory/Verbal Channel processes both auditory input (sounds) and verbal representation (printed words). The Visual Channel processes visual input and pictorial representations.

The caveat is that humans can only process a limited amount of information at any given time.

There is also a path that information takes as it leaves the outside world and enters your long term memory. That path starts with "Sensory Memory." What your eyes see and your ears hear.

From there, information flows to "Working Memory," where your "Cognitive Processing" happens. And if all goes well, new information gets retained in your "Long Term" memory.

THE CATCH

Here's the catch. Cognitive Processing happens in your Working Memory which can get easily overloaded. In fact, the estimate is that most people have a 20 second buffer in their working memory to correlate and store new information in their long term memory, or the information is lost.

WORDS ARE TRICKY

And now it gets tricky. When you hear words, you process what you hear in the Verbal Channel. When you see written words, you process these in the Verbal Channel too.

If we keep in mind that we have limited cognitive processing capability, then when we see a lot of words and hear a lot of words at the same time, a challenge to successful processing and integrating the information occurs. Especially when most people read faster than they can talk.

Mayer calls it "Cognitive Overload" when one or both channels are getting too much information. Turns out that humans don't retain the info. What that means is if you want to ensure that your audience doesn't "Get it," just read your slide. This was proven when narration matched the image (written words). Bottom Line: The same words written and spoken reduced retention and induced cognitive overload.

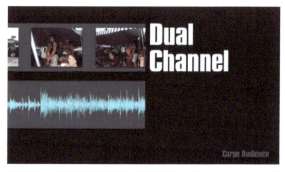

BAD, BAD COGNITIVE OVERLOAD

Cognitive overload in your audience is bad, bad, bad. What you've done is present more information than your audience can successfully process. When you have too many words on the screen, while at the same time saying those words, you lose your audience's attention. If you lose their attention, they quit learning. And they go away. Someplace in their mind where bad, bad, cognitive overload doesn't live. You know, the beach. And you just bought the audience a bus ticket. But, you've lost them. They are gone. And it's hard to get them back. Even with a margarita.

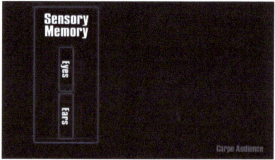

On the other hand, Mayer also proved that a relevant image in conjunction with narration improved retention. And for some topics, relevant animation enhanced learning.

At this point I'm going to bring Medina's work into the conversation. He has written a book with well researched, phenomenal insights: "Brain Rules." In it, he details 12 brain rules. While every one of them applies to giving better presentations, I'm going to focus on just a few of these rules.

> Rule #10: Vision wins.
> Rule #4: We don't pay attention to boring things.
>   *Rule #4 Corollary*: Emotions get our attention.
>   *Rule #4 Corollary*: 10 Minutes.
> Rule #5: Repeat to Remember.

VISION WINS

Medina spends some time talking about how important vision is and cites a number of studies on how it all works. Again, worth the read, but it might be covered by this simple question: "Why is there porn, if vision doesn't win?" Seriously, vision is so hard wired into human brains, that simply a picture of some naked person can invoke a physiological response. Vision wins. Case closed.

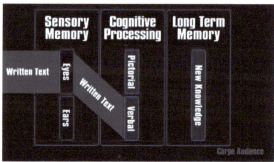

WE DON'T PAY ATTENTION TO BORING THINGS

Medina talks about boring: "You have only got seconds to grab someone's attention and only 10 minutes to keep it."

What's this mean for presentations? First, start with a bang. In presentations I make for The "I Love U Guys" Foundation I start with strong imagery and a quote.

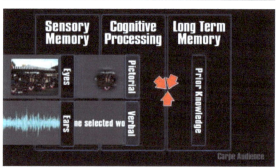

I am very cognizant of timing with this series of slides. While the images are sequencing I'm saying the quote. I am done talking when the text of the quote actually appears, so I

"

Peace

It does not mean to be in a place where there is no noise, trouble, or hard work.

It means to be in the midst of those things and still be calm in your heart.

"

pause, and let the audience read it again. Separate cognitive actions. Information delivered in two different ways, with images selected to evoke emotions. Emotions reinforced by the spoken word.

" The reality is that PowerPoint does **boring by default**."

You can see this isn't a typical PowerPoint. I'm using slides to support my presentation. The reality is that PowerPoint does "boring" by default. You have to override things to avoid boring. Remember PowerPoint coerces you into creating bullet lists. Always resist.

Starting a presentation with a quote can be the attention grabber you need to get things going. But don't simply show the words and read them. Give your audience strong visuals while you speak, then pause and let them read it themselves.

I also use the quote to close the presentation. It's a strong wrap to the presentation and gives the audience a clear end point.

EMOTIONS GET OUR ATTENTION

Medina continues with the assertion that emotionally arousing events tend to be better remembered than neutral events.

There is some frustration with this assertion because there is debate on what "exactly" an emotion is, but there is no doubt about the importance of emotion on learning. An emotionally charged event (or ECS, Emotionally Competent Stimulus) is the best-processed kind of external stimulus ever measured. Emotionally charged events persist much longer in our memories and are recalled with greater accuracy than neutral memories.[11]

This takes us to the simple question, "How do we introduce emotion into our presentations?" The answer is easy. Usually with pictures. Sometimes audio. Sometimes the story can be told with enough emotion to invoke it in the audience. But the simplest way is pictures.

PICTURES. LOTS OF PICTURES

Here's an example of how a few pictures can change the emotional tenor of a presentation. How a few pictures can transform a good conversation into a riveting one. A high school principal has given this presentation around the country. The call to action in this case was to remind administrators that no one is immune to school violence.

Part of the presentation was the narrative about the events that occurred over the course of a tragic afternoon at a rural high school in Colorado. Not a venue where you often see this level of first responder presence.

Take a look at the original blue screen slides below. Then at the images on the right. This is just a subset of the images used. They're timed to sequence automatically as the story is told. Is there any doubt that the story told over pictures has far more impact and than the story told over words?

School Crisis Leadership

- Summary of September 27th, 2006: A gunman entered the building and proceeded to room 206 where he held a College Preparatory English class hostage. He was armed with guns and stated that he had explosives. Over a period of approximately 5 hours, he released students through negotiations with the responding SWAT team. The gunman stated that it would be "all over at 4:00 p.m."

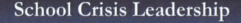

School Crisis Leadership

- Before 4:00, the SWAT team made up of an inter-jurisdictional force breached the room from 3 different vantage points and attempted to rescue two remaining hostages. The gunman turned the gun on himself after fatally wounding Emily Keyes, a 16 year old junior. He was also shot multiple times by the SWAT team.

Let's not forget that the little emotions are the great captains of our lives and we obey them without realizing it.

Vincent Van Gogh

THIS AIN'T MAIN STREET. IT'S HOLLYWOOD

As you look at the example slides in this book, you'll notice that there is an almost universal use of photos in one of three different layouts. The full screen image. The split screen image with type. And the single element on black. What you don't see are montages. You don't see tiny pictures (unless the visual goal is a contact sheet).

AUDIO, THE OTHER PROVOCATEUR

Sometimes audio can evoke emotion as well. I use 911 dispatch recordings when presenting on school safety. For other types of presentations I use iconic recordings from history. JFK, Martin Luther King, Reagan, Clinton. Or in the right context, sirens or simply crickets. Sometimes I have an image on screen with the audio. Sometimes a black screen with a short excerpt (seven words or less) to reinforce the point of the audio clip. It's really about garnering an emotion, to help the audience glue the information into their long term memory more efficiently.

THE 10 MINUTE BARRIER

The clock is ticking. Medina suggests that people (of all ages) have an attention span countdown. At 10 minutes, people start to look at the clock and wonder "When will this ever end?"

That means designing your presentation in 10 minute blocks. With starts and middles and ends. Medina says that you have to be careful with this though. You have to stay relevant. An irrelevant cue that takes them out of their current train of thought makes the information seem unorganized, disjointed or even patronizing and will infuriate your audience. His answer is to introduce something so compelling that they break through the 10 minute barrier. One strategy he suggests are "hooks." A wrap-up of what you just presented or a compelling intro about what comes next.

In a few pages we'll also look at other natural ways to leverage this 10 minute span. (Think evening news.)

REPEAT TO REMEMBER

Repetition is important. Not mindless boring repetition, but careful calculated repetition. Repetition where you say the same thing a few different ways. Or at different times. Or build on a concept. Or provide an analogy. Or deliver the opposite as well. When I say repetition is important, I'm not saying read what's written on your slide. That's the path to cognitive overload. I'm saying find ways to repeat the core messages, that support your call to action, in different ways.

At the very least, it's easy to restate a concept with the preface "Remember." Like this... Remember what Medina said? "Vision wins." And, "You have only got seconds to grab someone's attention and only 10 minutes to keep it."

WHO ARE THESE PEOPLE AND WHY ARE THEY HERE?

Sometimes it takes looking through the haze of campfire smoke to see the world clearly.

Author Unknown

CAMPFIRE THEORY

In order to give a compelling presentation you must first determine why people go to presentations. I think the first audience motivation is to be with folks that share the same experience, interest, vocation or speciality. It's about rubbing elbows with your peers. Telling stories and listening. It's about sitting around the metaphorical campfire and swapping yarns. (You know, Burning Man Lite, only with more clothes.)

That's really it. It's about the tribe you've chosen. Takes us to this declaration: "People attend your presentation to hear and watch 'you' tell your story." Not to read your slides. If folks wanted to read slides, then we wouldn't have conferences or meetings or classrooms. We'd just email our crappy PowerPoint back and forth.

" They want a **campfire** conversation, given by one of 'their' tribe.**"**

Why do they want to hear your story? Usually that's pretty simple. You're an expert. Or you have a compelling story. Or your product may solve a need. Or you have information that is important, scarce or new. Or you can debrief an incident or event. Or some combination of these. Whatever it is, your audience wants to hear you say it. And they may want to ask questions later. They want a campfire conversation, given by one of "their" tribe.

YOU HAVE THE TALKING STICK

The campfire conversation has a certain timing and delivery style. There are some audience preconceptions about a campfire conversation. First, you are handed the talking stick. And when you are holding the talking stick, folks shouldn't interrupt.

With campfire theory, your presentation is usually told as a story, or a series of stories. You might take the talking stick and draw in the sand around the fire-pit. (The first beta version of PowerPoint.) You may throw your hands in the air and dance around the fire as you tell it. Or you might stand at the edge and let the story float on its own.

Bottom line is that there is some element of performance in presentations, if you believe the campfire theory. Don't let this dissuade the novice or timid presenter. The performance part of a presentation is about the presenter. Your performance may be less animated. Don't stress. That's okay. It's still a campfire conversation if you tell stories. The joy of live stories from an audience perspective is that real people, of any exuberance level, can tell great stories.

THE SWEAT LODGE

There is another type of presentation. The board room. A very different type of presentation. Board rooms are about the metaphorical elders garnering information from the seekers and pathfinders. Typically, the metaphorical youth. I call it a sweat lodge presentation. You're given the talking stick, but you may be asked to hand it over now and again. In a board room presentation you may never even fire up a formalized PowerPoint presentation. Rather, you may have a number of visuals ready, but you need to design the presentation to support a random access into it. Think slide sorter.

The sweat lodge is more ad hoc. You have a theme, a direction and you best be ready to modify direction based on the "elders" moving the conversation. Cool. Embrace ad hoc.

> **"** But if the elders are **pesky,** be sure to have a transitional ending ready to go. **"**

The sweat lodge is about starting the conversation, but having a number of different transitions, in your pocket, ready to go. This is important. You also must have two endings. The first ending is the desired outcome. But if the elders are pesky, be sure to have a transitional ending ready to go. A transitional ending is one where you can see your ending down the road, but this ending is a starting point to get to your desired outcome.

Remember this though. The elders are there for a reason. They have knowledge and experience that may be outside of your direct experience. Pay close attention when the elders are reluctant to embrace your new goals.

AUDIENCE MATTERS

Before you begin to tell your story, you need to know who your audience is. This knowledge probably won't change the theme, but it certainly will impact how you tell your story, what specific jargon is used, what special skills are in play, and which parts of the story can be most effective for your audience. I do a lot of presentations on school safety. Sometimes to law enforcement only, sometimes to educators and administrators, sometimes to students. Sometimes combinations of the above. While every one of those roles has a stake in school safety, there are very different knowledge baselines represented.

I also give presentations to potential funders and contributors of the non-profit organization I work for. So I really have several distinct versions of my story, and a few more distinct combinations of my story. And I have different Keynote/PowerPoint presentations that support my telling of the story to different audiences within different time frames.

Your first presentation on a topic is probably to a known audience. If not, then find out. Call the host and ask about expectations, venue and considerations. Keep in mind, your presentation may be given again and again and again. Make sure you identify and accommodate the changing composition of your audience.

AUDIENCE CONDITIONING

There is another consideration about your audience. Every day they are subjected to "Presentation Conditioning." Here's what I mean. For adult audiences, the evening news is a presentation. And the presentation is given in a style with supporting graphics, images and multimedia. And that style rarely includes bullet lists or detailed graphs. (Even the weather map is simplified.) It is visually specific and relies on people (news anchors and reporters) to give the presentation. People telling their stories.

There is also a cadence involved. The short headline blurb. Transitions. The "in-depth" two to five minute report (which has its own internal cadence). Commercials and pauses. And this cadence, this timing, is important to observe and acknowledge.

> **"** Your audience is **conditioned** to receive information in this style with this cadence every day.**"**

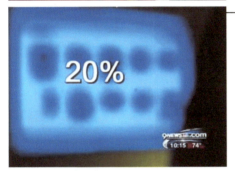

Because your audience is conditioned to receive information in this style with this cadence every day. And your audience has gotten good at it. If you base your style and timing on these proven techniques, you will leverage your audience's skill at consuming information in this manner.

For younger audiences, TV and internet are extremely influential in how kids get info. Watch a sitcom. Or a prime time cartoon. You'll see similar timing to the evening news. Short times, longer times, transitions, and breaks.

REMEMBER 10 MINUTES?

We can see one other factor at work with this cadence. The evening news is broken into about 8 minute segments with a couple of minutes of commercials at the end of each segment. Naturally resetting Medina's 10 minute clock.

What we're doing is setting the foundation for the structure of your presentation. Using principals of cognitive science, acknowledging that your presentation is really you telling stories to your audience, and structuring your stories to fit a known cadence, you will increase your audience's attention to you and your message.

Take a look at the screenshots. Notice that the "slides" are basic. "The Dangers of Sexting," or simply "20%".

SEE IT IN ACTION

Cementing the Audience Conditioning theory takes a clock and a legal pad. When you watch the news, jot down the headline and start time, including seconds. As transitions and breaks and commercials occur, jot down those times as well. Do that for a few broadcasts and compare timings. I'll call this the cadence of the program. And the cadence of your next presentation.

Also jot down the text and graphics used to support the telling of the story. Do the same for other types of broadcast media. Do it for half hour shows as well as hour long shows. The following charts show timelines of each piece of a typical half hour newscast.

THE FIRST 10 MINUTES (600 SECONDS)

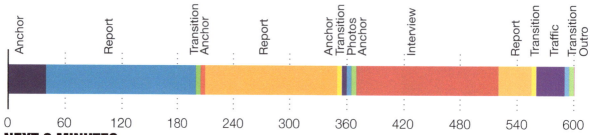

NEXT 2 MINUTES

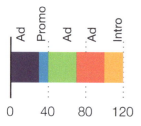

THE NEXT 10 MINUTES

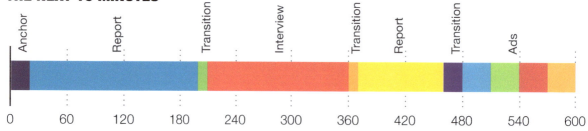

THE LAST 8 MINUTES

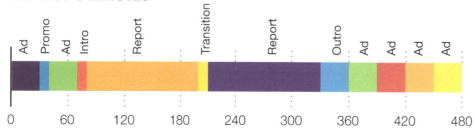

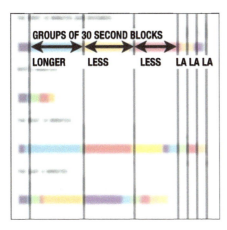

LEVERAGING THE 30 SECOND ATTENTION SPAN

If you squint a bit, you can see the pattern that our little graphing exercise reveals. It's really a pretty simple formula. At its core, it is based on 30 second building blocks with the occasional 10 second transition or reset. For reports and interviews, five to nine 30 second blocks are used. But even these have their own internal transitions and resets.

Let's call it the "30 Second Attention Span." In developing and ultimately delivering a presentation, the 30 second block is a barometer. And if you don't have a stopwatch on your phone, it's time to upgrade. Because you need to time things as you're developing your story.

Before you shout, "Lunatic! I can't tell anything in 30 seconds," don't stress. The 30 Second Attention Span is about developing your presen-

tation so that there is a logical transition/break/change at 30 seconds or so, to bring your audience back to your message. It may be a slide change. It may be a deliberate pause. It may be a shout. But whatever the device, it should be there. It's about truly, viscerally acknowledging, then fully leveraging, "Audience Conditioning," and building your presentation around it.

It's also about recognizing some other important presentation milestones. Somewhere in the 3 to 6 minute range you need to be finishing one story and starting the next. Because your audience is conditioned. And that is the "Cadence." Look at the graph to the left: "Longest, Less, Less... La, La, La." Rinse and repeat. (Occasionally an extra "La" or two sneaks in, but you get the idea.)

" I **heart** the Kool-Aid."

EMBRACE AND EXTEND

What's cool is that if you don't fight the 30 Second Attention Span, and rather assume it's real, then you may just change how you do other things beyond presentations. You see, I apply the 30 second rule to print media too. The layout of this book is an example. Notice the sub-heads and pull-out quotes. At average reading speeds, I break the text-flow with either a pullout or a sub head every 30 seconds. Really. (OK, Now you're going thumb through the book for a few seconds. See?) Same for reports, proposals and handouts. I've made this Kool-Aid and now I'm going to drink it. But it works. Try it. The next chapters talk about stories. And I'll be bringing the 30 Second Attention Span to the table with the crayons and napkins.

VISUAL SYNCOPATION

One more thing to pay attention to is what I call visual syncopation. That's where, over the course of your presentation, some rapid fire sequencing of your slides occur. Changing the pace is vital to keeping your audience's attention.

The following sequence is a segment of my Carpe Audience presentation. This segment happens early in the presentation. Notice this is the closest I get to my personal biography. I certainly don't start with that. I started with my outcomes. (Look at the narrative on the right.) The objectives of this part of the presentation are:

1. Establish basis of authority.
2. Show the audience a different look with PowerPoint and show them how I interact with visuals on screen. Learning by example is strong in humans, so my presentation is an ongoing example of the Carpe Way.
3. Introduce the notion that there is science behind my assertions.
4. Close with an engagement... You too can be "One in a Million."

Notice the slide durations. Total run time is just under a minute. There are some quick builds in here. If I'm on my game there are usually a couple of light chuckles over the course of this story.

Hi. Thank you. Today, I will reveal some of the secrets to giving better presentations even if you do use PowerPoint.

I'm also going to talk about some of the science behind how people learn. Human motivations. Brains. And some formulas that you can use immediately in your presentations. Formulas that work from the boardroom to the ballroom.

What we're not going to talk about is how to use PowerPoint. Effective business communication does not rely on your skills with PowerPoint. It relies on your understanding how humans learn.

Alright... Let's get started.

 **15 Seconds**	My day job used to be writing software, mostly behind corporate firewalls. Before that Graphic Design. I know, left brain, right brain... Shut up. In 2009 I made one of those mid life career changes. I signed on as Executive Director with a small non profit. One of the program development efforts was around school safety. So I ended up going to a ton of conferences. Symposiums, workshops and even board rooms. While I had seen plenty of bad PowerPoint in my corporate days, it was nothing compared to what I was seeing in the wild. Part of my role was "Outreach." So I also started to give presentations. And there was no way I was going to give dull, bad presentations. (Cuz, I've done that in the past. No way this time.)
 **3 seconds**	So I did some research. Hundreds of hours of research on how to give more effective presentations.
 **3 seconds**	I've also looked at dozens of self proclaimed experts. Like me. But most experts don't look at the science. They talk anecdotally. I do too.
 **5 seconds**	But I also point to clinical studies on how the mind learns new information. There are proven techniques that make your presentation better. And these techniques are important. Why?

3 seconds

It's said that there are over 30 Million PowerPoint presentations being given every day.

7 seconds w/pauses

Since this is one them, let's put that into perspective with a bar chart.

There.

30 Million.

One day.

5 seconds

More scale. There.

Not 10,
not 20,
but 30 Million...

3 seconds

Presentations.

And you know what?

2 seconds

29 Million suck.

3 seconds

That's a 97% suck factor.

Here's what's cool. That means...

5 seconds

...that 3% don't suck. A million great presentation are being given every day.

3 seconds

And I'm going to show you how you, too, can be "One in a Million."

EVERYTHING
IS A STORY.
EVERYTHING

If stories come to you, care for them.

And learn to give them away where they are needed.

Sometimes a person needs a story more than food to stay alive.

Barry Lopez

EVERYTHING IS A STORY. EVERYTHING

Crikey. Over three dozen pages in and we haven't even cracked open PointPoint or done a really cool curvy arrow or animated transition. That's because those things rarely matter. What matters are the stories. Stories in time. Stories of circumstance. Stories of purpose. Your PowerPoint slides should be supporting your stories, not telling them. So, find your stories and the slides will beat a path to your door. (Or at least appear on a napkin.)

When I say everything is a story, that's precisely what I mean. The pie chart is a story. Your introduction is a story. Every fact presented is a story. Every anecdote is a story. Your presentation is a chain of stories.

Now, you may not have thought of a pie chart as a story, but for presentation development we're going to consider it a story. It may be a short story. "Just the facts ma'am." Or you may want to isolate a data point and humanize it. With The "I Love U Guys" Foundation, we are working to bring a safety protocol to every school in the country,[12] starting in Colorado. At the time of this writing, the program was in 35% of the public K-12 schools in the state. As the slide was shown, I gave the basic stats, and then dropped into an experience I had when visiting one of those schools.

" You need an **end game**. First. "

SAY NOTHING WITHOUT A PURPOSE

Telling stories is usually not enough though. Each of your stories must be measured by what you want your audience to get from this story. Means that you need an end game. First.

It's the "call to action." If the people in your audience were programmable what would it look like when you gave the presentation?

   Step 1: See Presentation.
   Step 2: Do Something.

What is that something? When you are done with your presentation, what is the call to action? What is the desired outcome? What do you want tomorrow's water-cooler conversation to include about your presentation?

The call to action is imperative. It's probably your "close." It's how the audience can embrace your message, share your goals, buy your product, learn a lesson, debrief or take your message to others. Don't be shy about having a couple of calls to action. Often change is a process, not a switch, so provide incremental actions based on either enthusiasm level or role.

And don't be shy about introducing affiliates, partners or other organizations that support your action. I'm not talking about competitors, but other entities that share the space.

I've also seen several powerful, emotional, heartfelt presentations that have ended without a call to action. Or the call to action was to book the presentation. But that's a different story. (Oh... That reminds me. If you want to book the Carpe Audience Presentation for your company, school, or organization, email: booking@carpeaudience.com.)

Without the call to action, those stories, while emotional, weren't fulfilling. And in fact, they either left me drained or bummed. Neither of which is an outcome that seems desired.

So write it down. "I want my audience to do this…"

STARTING FROM THE END

So, when you are putting your presentation together, you are starting from the end. You are using the philosophy that the first goal of your presentation is to support the call to action. Different story components then directly support the call to action, provide valuable background info, set the stage, or are a break or transition.

As you prepare your stories and later develop your Keynote/PowerPoint, each paragraph of every story and ultimately every slide should be side-noted with which type of story you are telling. Here's why: Often you end up with a presentation that gets used multiple times. Under different time constraints. By side noting each paragraph you can prioritize which story components get used or not.

You might develop your story as an outline. (A hidden bullet list.) That's fine. It's your story writing style. Keep in mind your bullet lists are stories. Sometimes one story. Sometimes many.

THE PEN IS MIGHTIER THAN THE MOUSE. UNTIL IT ISN'T

I start any new presentation with old school tools. A legal pad and a pen. (I want to see my scratch outs.) Later I'll migrate to a text editor, or a simple page layout word processor. But the legal pad is essential. Perhaps for a less obvious reason – focus.

" Medina and others say that
   multi-tasking **is a myth**."

Medina and others say that multi-tasking is a myth. So I take my legal pad to the couch. Or the coffee shop. But away from email and chat and the office phone and any other professional distraction. I put the time I'm going to work on the presentation on my calendar, as if it were a meeting. In a sense, it is. It's a meeting of one, with similar protocols. No interruptions, please.

BACK TO THE END

Knowing the call to action is essential. But it might be more difficult than you think to actually define it. An event debriefing may give an audience information on how the presenter acted during the event, with the ultimate call to action being, "Take these experiences, evaluate your practices against this information and if needed modify your practice." Or, perhaps it's a sales presentation and the call to action is the next step in the sales cycle. Or, it's new information where the call to action is after the presentation, dig in and do some homework.

No, it's not a very good story…
its author was too busy listening to other voices to listen as closely as he should have to the one coming from inside.

Stephen King

Time	Story	Type	Slide
0:00:10	Intro	Transition	Howdy
0:00:20			
0:00:30	Peace	Set the Stage	Peace
0:00:40			Images
0:00:50			Quote
0:01:00			
0:01:10			
0:01:20	About	Set the Stage	Not Easy
0:01:30			
0:01:40			
0:01:50			
0:02:00			
0:02:10			
0:02:20			
0:02:30			
0:02:40			
0:02:50			
0:03:00			
0:03:10			
0:03:20	Stand Up	Call to Action	Not Me
0:03:30			
0:03:40			
0:03:50	Legal Pad		
0:04:00			
0:04:10			
0:04:20			
0:04:30	Kids	Background	Not Said
0:04:40			
0:04:50			
0:05:00			
0:05:10			
0:05:20			
0:05:30			
0:05:40			
0:05:50	How Many	Transition	Zero
0:06:00			Hundreds
0:06:10	Media	Set the Stage	10 Years
0:06:20			
0:06:30			
0:06:40			
0:06:50			
0:07:00			
0:07:10			
0:07:20			
0:07:30			
0:07:40			
0:07:50			
0:08:00			
0:08:10			
0:08:20			
0:08:30			
0:08:40			
0:08:50			
0:09:00			
0:09:10			
0:09:20	Stats	Call to Action	300 Million
0:09:30	Safe2Tell	Call to Action	Can't Stop
0:09:40		Call to Action	Wrong
0:09:50		Background	Stats
0:10:00	Story	Background	9:23 AM

WRITING THE STORY

When you are writing your presentation you're really writing a handful of little stories that share a theme and support your call to action. With some stories it may be a creative process to form the words. A personal experience that needs to be told. In others, it may be organizational. For instance a timeline. This happened, then this happened. Or it may simply be a statement of fact or result of research.

For creating the stories, my style is to write the story out most of the time. Sentences and paragraphs. Sometimes I'll put together a conversational outline (for my own reference, not the screen) so I remember to hit all relevant points. But usually I'll write it out as if I were going to present it exactly as written.

The point is that I end up with a collection of stories and facts all written down. Some may not be totally complete, but the bulk of it is there. Notice, I haven't even fired up my presentation software, or made a single slide.

SEQUENCING

Once you've written (or outlined) your story, it's time to break it down and identify story components. Remember our story types? (Call to Action, Background Fact, Set the Stage, Break, Transition.) Why is this important? A few reasons. First, it helps you separate conversation blocks into types. Furthermore, it allows you to begin to manage the cadence of the presentation.

Where transitions need to happen. What blocks are for which audiences. When you need to shorten your presentation, it may help you prioritize what stays and what goes. It's also useful when you see what background or factual data needs to be presented prior to reference of that information.

Here's how I do it. I take each paragraph (or outline group) and read or practice it. With a stop watch. Next to the paragraph I put down the time. I also try to identify the story component type. Is this paragraph part of the story of the last paragraph? Or is it a transition into a new story?

Somewhere along the way, I've usually transitioned from paper to digital. For me it's a text editor. A word processor is just fine too.

You might liken it to a script, and if the power went out at your presentation it very well could be. But, it's also your timing guide. Take your stories and see how they fit into the Cadence.

CREATE A CADENCE WORKSHEET

On the left is a sample of a cadence worksheet created in a spreadsheet program. It has 10 second intervals on the left and Story Name, Type and what's on the slide on the right. Use this to start sequencing your assorted stories.

Try to focus on 10 minute blocks. For each block you should end up with about three 2 to 5 minute stories. Then, with transitions and intros you naturally achieve 10 minutes.

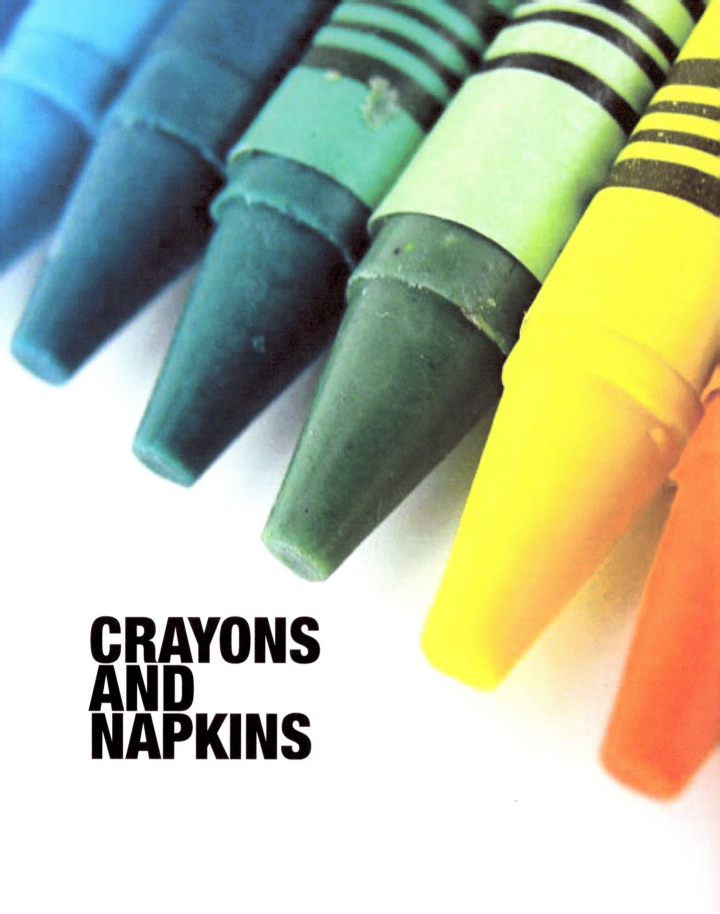

CRAYONS
AND
NAPKINS

> "
> I'll try anything once, twice if I like it, three times to make sure.
> "
>
> *Mae West*

YOU REALLY NEED TO DO THIS

This is an exercise. Do it at least once. More if you need to. Here's how it works. Once you have your basic presentation written and sequenced, grab a pile of napkins and a box of crayons. With each of your stories, take a napkin and write with a crayon what should be on a slide, to support your story.

Maybe it's a picture. Maybe it's a word or seven. What ever it is, write it on the napkin with crayon.

Two more rules. You can't hold your crayon like a pencil. Rather, make a fist and hold the crayon with the point coming out by your pinkie. And... If you tear the napkin, with the crayon, while you're writing, the slide was too complicated. Start over.

BARS AND TALKING STICKS

Think of it this way... If you were at an airport bar and a conversation evolved about your passion, what would you do? Remember, if we were around the campfire, you would use the talking stick to draw in the sand. But you're not there, you're in a bar. A kid friendly bar. So they have crayons. And napkins. And you're holding your beer in the same hand, which is why you're holding the crayon with the point by your pinkie. (You have the bottom of the beer glass clenched firmly with your index finger and thumb. And you're holding the napkin down with your other hand.) Carpe Audience.

Wait a second, why not just use a pen? Seriously, you just try to borrow a pen from an airport bartender.

Here's the point. PowerPoint is designed to degrade your stories, your presentation, your passion, into bullet lists. By knowing in advance, what your slide says, or what the image is, you can defeat the PowerPoint bullet list generation algorithms.

Another outcome of this exercise is that after just a little bit, you begin to understand the essence of your story.

Here's an example. In one of my presentations, I cycle through the following three slides as I tell a couple of stories. Actual runtime of this conversational sequence is about three to four minutes. During the "Not Me" slide I actually do a little audience participation moment. This has proven to be a pretty powerful segment and it was first revealed with crayons and napkins.

 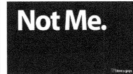 

ONE MORE THING

There's no science here... just speculation. When you grab a crayon, and hold it with your fist, you're three years old again. And the smell of the crayon and the gentleness of trying not to tear the napkin, might just combine to let your youthful primitive write what needs to be written.

WHILE THE CRAYONS ARE STILL HOT

If you really raided the cupboard or pantry and got out a stack of napkins, and raided the kids' room and got out the crayons, and really tried to write on napkins with crayons, then you discovered the most important secret to giving better presentations: "No more than seven words per slide." Yes, slide.

Now, some folks[13] say only six words per slide. But then you would need two slides for the rule. I like seven. It's the Carpe way. There is an exception... Quotes. But even then there is a rule. If you put more than seven words on a slide, stop talking. Instead, when the slide first appears, read it to yourself. Read halfway through again before you start talking. What I'm saying here is reduce the cognitive load. Let your your audience read at their own pace. And shut up while they're doing it.

The other exception might be a graph. But almost universally, no more than seven words on a slide.

POWERPOINT RULES OF THUMB AND OTHER THINGS THAT ARE INCREDIBLY STUPID

If you search for "PowerPoint Rules of Thumb," a few things bubble up pretty quickly. I'll start with the "Rule of Six," There are others though.

" Snagged their **curly** hooks..."

Oddly, it makes me really curious how these presentation memes have snagged their curly hooks into the cultural DNA of PowerPoint presentations. But they have.

Smart people have stood red-faced and shouting defending some of these rules. But they are wrong. They've mistaken intent. Your slides aren't a teleprompter. Not a handout. Not your presentation. (See O'Henry.) Your slides are scratches in the sand, drawn ad hoc while you tell a campfire story.

So. Let's look at some of these prognostications with a titter in our throats.

THE STUPID RULE OF SIX

There are variations on this one, but basically the rule of six goes like this... "No more than six lines per slide, and no more than six words per line." Whoever came up with this one clearly didn't base it on any sort of scientific approach to presentation design or delivery. But this one is pervasive. And it's really stupid. The only time you should employ this rule is when you want to hide the truth. Or make sure your audience doesn't remember it. Or when you want to induce early sleep. Because if you employ this rule, and then read your slide, you will induce cognitive overload. Not "might" induce. You will. Remember, cognitive overload is bad, bad, bad. It's hard to get them back from the beach, once you give them the bus ticket.

The rule of six is about confusing PowerPoint with a desktop publishing program. Your slide is there to support your conversation with your audience. Not have it.

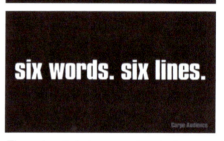

The rule of six is pervasive, but wrong. It is a sure path to cognitive overload.

OK, what's the plural? Is it rules of thumb or rule of thumbs?

Malcolm Lazlow

THE STUPID TWO MINUTE RULE

Here's another one. No more than one slide per two minutes. I think that rule was written by someone who stops to read billboards, has never seen television, and doesn't own a clicker. You absolutely must include some rapid fire sequencing over the course of your presentation. When I'm slide burning, I'll run three or four or even five sequential slides over the course of six to eight seconds. I'll pause on the next to let us all catch our breath. Remember Cadence and the evening news.

Remember Mayer's research? "People learn more deeply from words and pictures than from words alone."

I can guarantee you this. If you have three solid images, or three solid numbers, or three solid words, rapid sequencing will increase audience attention and retention when you click your way through them as you speak. Doesn't mean that you don't need to practice this technique. Because you do. But if you nail it... Carpe Audience.

THE STUPID 36 POINT, FONT SIZE RULE

I said it earlier, if your presentation was a newspaper, your slide is the headline and you are the story. And baby, when you're giving a presentation, you are the front page. You tell me whether or not you're above the fold. Think bigger. Hundreds of points bigger.

STUPID, STUPID CLIP ART

Free up some space on your hard drive. Just erase the clip art that came with PowerPoint. Seriously, you should never ever use it. Just get rid of it. There is no emotional hook, no communication benefit, no humor, no sorrow, no graphical relevance, no benefit in using a a poorly drawn, not quite a cartoon, color blobby thing on your slide. None. Really.

Think pictures.

STUPID, STUPID, STUPID BULLET POINTS

This takes us back to the "Rule of Six." Most presentations that use lengthy bullet lists typically aren't effective. The real challenge is how to present sequential information in a manner that keeps the audience's interest. Read on and learn the Power List.

MORE STUPID: TITLE ALL OF YOUR SLIDES WITH A HEADING

There is a school of thought that says put a title on your slides. Why. Really, why? Your slides aren't a book. Your slides aren't a teleprompter. You are telling a story.

THE WORDS "IN SUMMARY" MEAN "OH, THANK GOD IT'S OVER"

Somewhere out there is the "In Summary..." school. You know, tell them what you told them. Summaries are for the weak. You weren't able to invoke the call to action, so here's your last ditch effort. Again, you tell me. One presenter says, "In summary, blah blah blah." The other says, "Before we wrap, I want to share one more cool thing, and we talked about it earlier..."

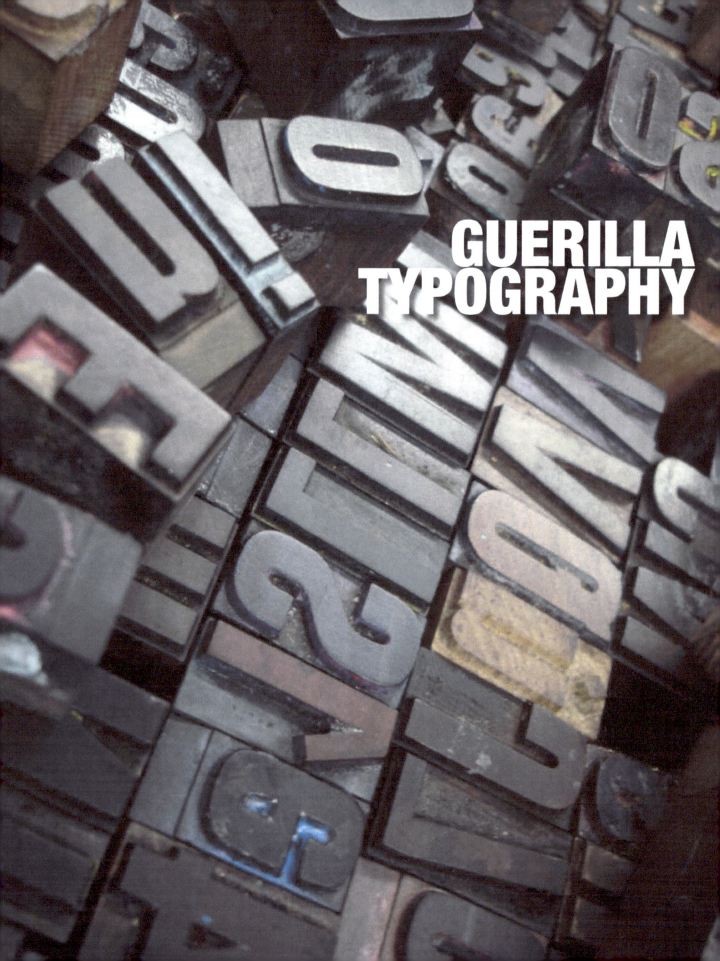

GUERILLA TYPOGRAPHY

"
Typography
has one
plain duty
before it
and that is
to convey
information
in writing.
"

Emil Ruder

GUERILLA TYPOGRAPHY

Fonts are the core of graphic communication. Creating a great presentation means that you need to introduce a little typography into your presentation visuals. Not type, but the art form of typography.

This section of the book won't make you a typographer. But it will reveal a handful of secrets to make your text look better. These aren't hard. In fact, most are easy. The hardest part about using these secrets is not believing defaults.

By default, PowerPoint gives you crap. Times Roman. Now, don't get me wrong, Times Roman has its place. But not usually in a presentation. PowerPoint also defaults to very open line spacing. These defaults were designed by programmers. Not typographers. They are wrong. Repeat and understand... The defaults are wrong.

CONSISTENCY IS CRITICAL

There is one other secret to typography. Consistency. Consistent positioning. Consistent use of upper, lower and mixed case. Consistent font selection and font size. For presentations, guerilla typography starts by selecting two or three font sizes that you will use in your presentation. Not two or three fonts. Just one font, in two or three sizes. As you're creating slides, your layouts need to share size and location between layouts.

"AutoFit is **evil**."

By default, PowerPoint thwarts your efforts to keep positioning and size consistent. Out of the box, PowerPoint has a clever "feature" called AutoFit. And AutoFit is evil. If your headline is too long for the line, AutoFit starts reducing your type size and changing the baseline position of the text box. Clearly, the secret of consistency remains secret to the engineers at Microsoft.

The back of this section has some How-to tips on changing this default behavior, as well as how to implement some of the techniques necessary in achieving guerilla typography. Again, repeat and understand... The defaults are wrong.

THE GUERILLA RECIPE

The recipe for better looking slides is simple:
1. Be consistent.
2. Select a sans-serif, bold, black font with a tall x-height.
3. Tighten your kerning
4. Reduce your leading.

Consistent also means no shouting. Don't throw an all-cap word in for EMPHASIS. You have a voice. That's where emphasis lives. Think headlines. Not necessarily tabloids.

The other consideration is that for slides, we're talking headlines. Not blocks of copy. This installment of guerilla typography is all about headlines. To understand the recipe, we need a quick primer on typography. (Skip this if your kerning is right, your leading is tight and your x-heights are high.)

FONT TYPES

Let's start with the basics, Serif and Sans-Serif. In French "Serif means 'Foot.' Sans means 'Without' - So, Sans-Serif is without feet." What's that mean? Sans-Serif fonts don't have little doodlies sticking out.

Serif
Times New Roman

> **Doodlies**

> **No Doodlies**

Sans-Serif
Helvetica Neue Regular

There are also derivatives. For instance, Look at this Slab Serif font.

Slab Serif
PT Barnum

> **Square Doodlies**

Then there are Scripts, Decoratives and Old English Stuff. Which usually never, ever get used in a presentation.

Scripts
Snell Roundhand Bold

> **Wedding Invitation**

Decoratives
Old Dreadful No. 7

> **Dreadful Indeed**

Old English
Engravers' Old English

> **Diplomas**

First Rule of Thumb. Always use a sans-serif font. Period. It's faster and easier to read. Less screen noise.

HELVETICA - THE MOVIE

For the over achiever, there's actually a pretty good film. The description from the website reads:

Helvetica *is a feature-length independent film about typography, graphic design and global visual culture. It looks at the proliferation of one typeface (which recently celebrated its 50th birthday in 2007) as part of a larger conversation about the way type affects our lives.*

http://helveticafilm.com

FONT WEIGHT

A font family usually has variations on the font design regarding the thickness of the characters. This is referred to as the "Weight" of the font. Here are some examples

Ultra Light
Helvetica Neue Ultra Light

Light
Helvetica Neue Light

Regular
Helvetica Neue Regular

Medium
Helvetica Neue Medium

Bold
Helvetica Neue Bold

Condensed Bold
Helvetica Neue Condensed Bold

Condensed Black
Helvetica Neue Condensed Black

For example purposes, here is a sample of a similar face with a "black" weight.

Black
Arial Black

FONT MEASUREMENTS

Font measurement is the next aspect of typography. Recognize that some of these measurements are relative to the font face being used. The first font displayed is Helvetica Neue Regular, the second font is Commador Extended and the third font displayed is Garamond. Notice the difference in the X-height, Ascender and Descender heights.

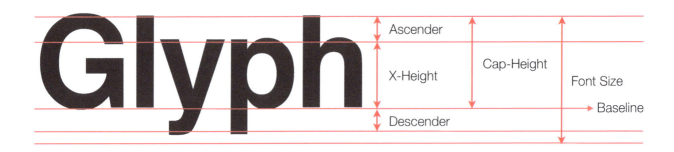

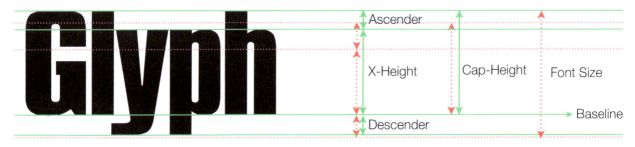

Notice that the X-height is much taller with this face compared to the original. And finally look at the X-height of the font below.

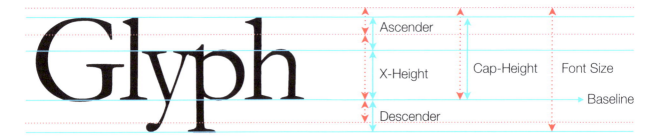

Finally, look at the x's below. They are all the same font size, 96pt.

COMMON KERNING PAIRS

While not at all inclusive, here is a list of some common kerning pairs. Keep in mind that every typeface, even every size is different. What may need kerning in Helvetica may be just fine in Verdana.

AC	LV	Va	dd	ov
AG	LW	Ve	dv	ow
AO	LY	Vi	dw	ox
AQ	Ly	Vo	dy	oy
AT	NA	Vu	eb	py
AU	OA	WA	eg	ra
AV	OT	WO	ep	rc
AW	OV	Wa	ev	rd
AY	OW	We	ew	re
Ap	OX	Wh	ex	rg
Au	OY	Wi	ey	ri
Av	PA	Wo	fa	rk
Aw	Pa	Wu	fe	rl
Ay	Pe	Wy	ff	rm
BA	Po	YA	fi	rn
BU	QU	YO	fl	ro
DA	RO	Ya	fo	rp
DV	RT	Ye	ga	rq
DW	RU	Yi	ge	rr
DY	RV	Yo	gg	rs
FA	RW	Yu	gi	rt
Fa	RY	ab	go	ru
Fe	TA	ag	gr	rv
Fi	TO	ap	gy	ry
Fo	Ta	at	hy	sw
Fr	Te	av	iv	va
JA	Th	aw	ke	ve
Ja	Ti	ay	ko	vo
Je	To	bb	ky	wa
Jo	Tr	bl	lw	we
Ju	Tu	bu	ly	wh
KO	Tw	bv	mu	wo
Ke	Ty	by	my	xe
Ko	UA	ch	nu	ya
Ku	VA	ck	nv	ye
Ky	VG	cl	ny	yo
LT	VO	cy	og	ze

KERNING

Kerning is the act of adjusting letter spacing between two characters to create a more "Balanced" presentation of white space.

Not to be confused with "tracking," which is adjusting the space between all of the characters uniformly.

Here's an example. In the word "Aviator" below, the letter spacing is identical.

But when you look at it, we really need to adjust some of the letter spacing.

Notice below how the white space between characters looks more "balanced."

Kerning only takes a moment and is an essential aspect of producing good looking slides.

TRACKING

Tracking is adjusting the spacing between letters uniformly. In the following examples both tracking and kerning have been applied.

LEADING

Leading is the typographical term for "Line Spacing." Again the defaults are not about typography but about safe and vanilla. If you look at the following, the line spacing is set at the default, but is really too spaced out. And the font is Times Roman.

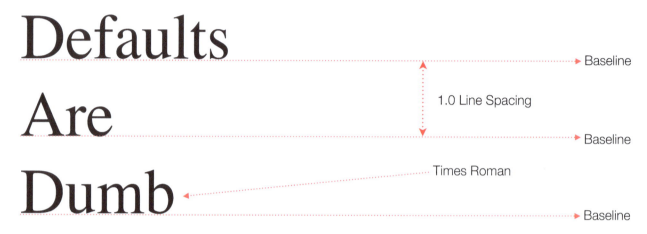

What needs to happen is to override the defaults and turn your airy headline into a tight headline. We're also going to select Helvetica Neue Condensed Bold. Here's what it looks like:

APPLIED KNOWLEDGE

Why did we do that? With what we gleaned from multimedia learning and our quick survey on type faces, when you are selecting a font for your presentation you absolutely must choose a sans-serif face. It's about cognitive overload. Serif faces have all of those little doodlies. More visual noise on screen. Think of your presentation as a newspaper. Your slide is the headline. And you are the story. So choose a sans-serif font.

Next is font weight... Bold. Condensed Bold. Black and Condensed Black. Those form your palette. That's really it. Guerilla Typography can be summed up by choosing a condensed bold or black face with a tall x-height, tightening your line spacing, reduce your letter spacing and pay attention to kerning.

USING ALL CAPS MAY LOOK TIGHT

But mixed or lower case might read better.

You make the call.

> " **Guerilla Typography** is simple: Choose a condensed bold or black face with a tall x-height, tighten your line spacing, reduce your letter spacing and pay attention to kerning."

TO CAP OR NOT TO CAP

I have a mixed mind on whether or not to run all caps in a presentation. Stylistically, it can be visually compelling. Tightly leaded, all cap blobs of text littering the screen. But, there is also research that indicates legibility, hence rapid understanding increases with mixed and lower case.

FINDING FREE FONTS

We live in amazing times. The quality and availability of free fonts, online, is profound. One of my favorite sites is http://dafont.com. There are others - http://fontsquirrel.com and http://1001fonts.com come to mind. Remember that there are considerations and risks associated with using non standard fonts. Missing typefaces are a real bummer. So, you must either run your presentation from your own machine, or you must package your presentation using the "Embed Fonts" option in PowerPoint. It's not a bad idea to keep a copy of your non-standard fonts in your presentation folder.

http://dafont.com   http://fontsquirrel.com   http://1001fonts.com

SPELL CHECK

One more consideration with typography sounds simple. In 2003, this internet meme started to float around. Read the following paragraph.

Aoccdrnig to a rscheearch at Cmabrigde Uinervtisy, it deosn't mttaer in waht oredr the ltteers in a wrod are, the olny iprmoetnt tihng is taht the frist and lsat ltteer be at the rghit pclae. The rset can be a toatl mses and you can sitll raed it wouthit porbelm. Tihs is bcuseae the huamn mnid deos not raed ervey lteter by istlef, but the wrod as a wlohe.

Turns out that this didn't happen at Cambridge and is an edge example, not actually an accurate, universal rule. Matt Davis of Cambridge[14] cites Graham Rawlinson's work in this area. But it does illustrate that while your audience might get what's on a slide, even if it's not spelled correctly, don't make them work for it. Spell check is good.

HOW TO: FIXING POWERPOINT DEFAULTS

There are some really aggravating defaults that PowerPoint uses out of the box. Remedy starts by getting into the right options.

Once you're in the PowerPoint Options dialog box, select proofing and click on "AutoCorrect Options."

The next dialog is where some of the Auto-Irritate "Features" live. Starting with the AutoCorrect Tab, I deselect all of the options presented. They are pretty self explanatory, but my preference is to choose to be responsible for what I type. (But I absolutely still spell check.)

The next tab is "AutoFormat As You Type," and positioning and size mischief lives here. It's called "AutoFit" and what it does is change the size and/or position of type in placeholders rather than wrapping to the next line. While you're down there, uncheck Automatic Bulleted Lists too. Really.

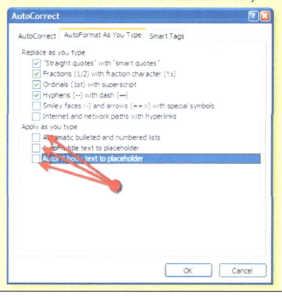

HOW TO: KERNING IN POWERPOINT

To kern a character pair in PowerPoint, select the first character and right click. You'll be presented the following sub menu.

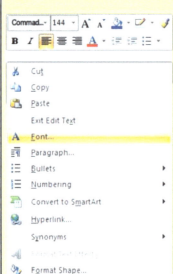

Select "Font," choose the character spacing tab and you'll see the following dialog.

Notice the spacing drop down has been set to "Condensed."

HOW TO: KERNING IN KEYNOTE

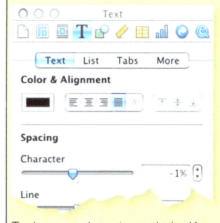

To kern a character pair in Keynote, show the Text Inspector and select the first character of the kerning pair you want to adjust. Slide the character spacing slider.

HOW TO: LEADING IN WINDOWS POWERPOINT

To modify line spacing in PowerPoint, select the text placeholder and right click. You'll be presented the following sub menu.

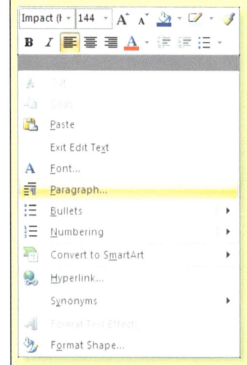

Select "Paragraph" and you'll see the following dialog.

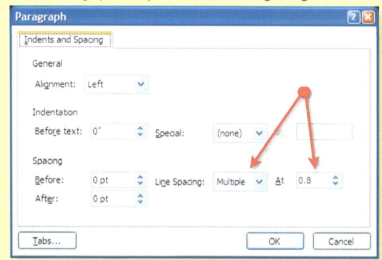

Notice in the middle of the "Spacing" section that "Line Spacing" has been set to "Multiple" and the "At" value is set to 0.8.

This setting will reduce the line spacing by 20%.

HOW TO: LEADING IN APPLE KEYNOTE

To modify line spacing in Keynote, show the Text Inspector and select the line of text you want to adjust. Slide the line spacing slider or enter decimal values into the data entry field.

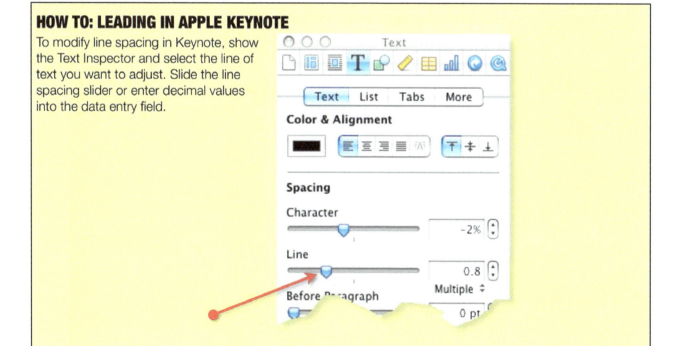

SIGNAL TO
NOISE RATIO

> It's simple,
> if it jiggles,
> it's fat.

Arnold Schwarzenegger

UNSUCKING YOUR TEMPLATES

Most templates suck. Seriously, look at 'em. Clearly Microsoft committed no expense to design. Bad fonts. Bad backgrounds. Bad samples. Bad defaults. Just bad. Kack. Stock templates are a guaranteed way to decrease your presentation's effectiveness.

Here's the deal. I don't think clouds help your presentation. Or... While those two pastel lines are precisely placed and tasteful in their nature, combining them with "squares of randomness," is quite simply unnecessary, noisy, ill-conceived, distracting, slightly off from true stylistic perfection, and stupid. I've even seen where a presenter had her photo on every slide as part of the template. (Her reasoning? "Well, it's a webinar, I wanted to make human contact.)

The benefit of a template is consistency. Type and images appear in the same place between slides. Font usage and size are consistent. (Remember, you need to reset your defaults!) But, I just said the default templates suck. Yes. They do. You need to create a template. And your template has about four, and no more than six, individual slide layouts.

SIGNAL TO NOISE RATIO

It all comes back to noise. All that clutter in the background increases the visual noise and begins to occlude the signal. You're including little line-drawn bubbles to make your slides less boring? Explain that to me. The whole point of the Carpe Way is to reduce the noise so your message gets heard.

BACKGROUNDS

Your background should be simple. I like black. Solid black. For a while, I liked a graduated background, black to dark grey or blue-grey. But I've been burned by graduated backgrounds. (Especially in webinars. Set your display to 256 colors and watch what happens to your graduated background.) The predictability of a graduated background varies on equipment. Lose that variable.

The other choice is of course, white. I have been in some high ambient light venues where black on a white background may have increased visibility. Yet, I still prefer a solid black background. Less likely to induce tanned retinas.

BLACK. LIKE THE NIGHT. WHERE CAMPFIRES LIVE

Why black? It's theatrical. With white type, it's contrasty. It isn't blue. It migrates well. Black backgrounds with white type are predictable. I know what it looks like in person or on a monitor or on a TV or an iPhone or an iPad. It also gets totally mashed up when I use the "Print Handout" option. Which at first glance might sound like a show-stopper, but is really a reminder that handouts printed from your slide show are a real no-no. (See Handout Theory.)

The bottom line is that the simpler the background, the greater the focus on the foreground. Don't distract your audience with tacky, vanilla, over-used, squares-of-randomness, generic backgrounds. Just lose them.

BACK TO TEMPLATES - YOUR LOGO

Here's one that is fraught with controversy. Some presentation pros are adamant, "Putting your logo on every slide is dumb," they proclaim. Others say just the opposite. For this one, you could defer to the evening news. Usually, they put their logo on every screen.

This is a fun slide. During my Carpe Audience presentation I bring up "the campfire theory" text. Soon it catches fire. Here's the fun part... Very quietly, with a gradual fade in, crickets begin chirping. Sometimes I move around and rub my eyes, as if virtual smoke is following me. Other times I might warm my hands over the projected fire. All the time, I share the campfire theory of presentation participation.

"**Lose** the clutter."

On the other hand, Garr Reynolds says simply "Lose the clutter." There's a lot to be said about that.

If you do decide to put your logo on every slide, then because we're using a black background, this means that you need to find or create the "Reverse" version of your logo. And make sure the background is transparent. Place the logo on your master slide layouts.

It's not acceptable to use your normal logo in a little white box. Just isn't. We're looking for excellence. Your master layout templates only need to be done once. Do them right.

Placement? Lower left or lower right. When I do use a logo, I almost universally place the logo lower right. Put it on all of your template slides but one. You need to have a totally blank slide, usually for multimedia clips. It's important that you also verify that the position of the logo is identical on all slides. As you are going through your presentation, using different layouts, the logo can't be dancing and moving and shaking around.

Or just listen to Garr and lose the clutter.

Many are
stubborn in
pursuit of the
path they have
chosen, few in
pursuit of
the goal.

Friedrich Nietzsche

ASPECT RATIO

It's a high definition world out there. I've been producing and presenting using an 16 x 9 720 HD format. My own projector is at a resolution of 1280 x 800, and letterboxes my presentation to 1280 x 720. I like the higher resolution and format. Again we're conditioned by that aspect ratio. It's more theatrical. It's higher quality. But there are costs.

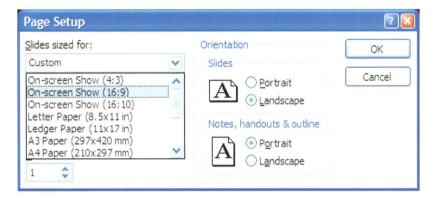

In the beginning most projectors were at a resolution of 800 x 600, which is an aspect ratio of 4 x 3. But things have changed. Almost all computer monitors and televisions being sold today are wide screen. Somewhere around a 16 x 9 aspect ratio.

Most business projectors are still at that 4 x 3 aspect ratio, but if you look at home theater projectors there are full HD 1920 x 1080 models for under a grand. (We live in amazing times.) So, in the next year or so, I'll probably migrate to full 1080 HD presentations.

Like I said, there are costs. First, I have to retool my presentations to get them on an iPad. Bummer. PowerPoint sometimes tries to reformat the presentation to a 4 x 3 aspect ratio, which of course, makes me curse. Some old projectors might balk at displaying correctly. (Nothing worse than anamorphic scaling.)

Despite the fact that it is absolutely more work, I still like the HD look and continue to develop in HD. Your mileage may vary.

TEMPLATE DESIGNS - THREE OR FOUR OR FIVE OR SIX

The final part of template design is creating a big text template slide. A medium text template slide. An image only template slide and a combination image / text slide.

Erase all bullet list templates. (We'll build one power-list template for the occasional highlight oriented conversation.)

You also need a totally blank template slide and a logo only template slide.

As you are creating the template slides, you also should modify the slide transition. For "Keynote" on the Mac, set the slide transition to dissolve. For "PowerPoint" set the slide transition to fade. Transition time in both cases should be at .5 to 1 seconds.

BLACK AND WHITE

I can't emphasize strongly enough keeping your backgrounds black and your type white. There may be opportunities for shades of grey and occasionally color. But if you stick with black and white, then, when you use color it will have impact.

MASTER TEMPLATES

You can see the evolution of master slides, moving from the default Blank Template when you create a new presentation in PowerPoint, to where your master slides are trimmed to the bare minimum.

Remember the defaults are wrong. We've changed the aspect ratio, using page setup, background and type colors were modified, and the bulk of the layouts have been deleted.

It's also important to point out that the text boxes have been set in the master template to align top and align left.

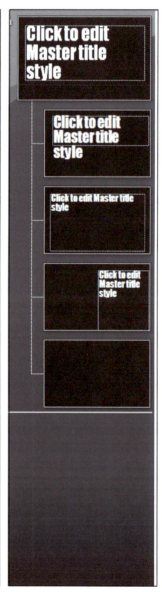

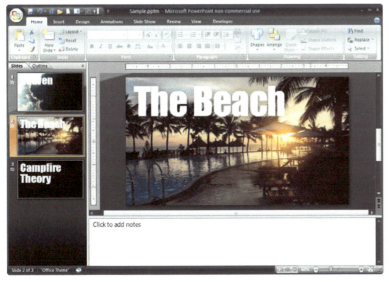

FORMAT TEXT EFFECTS

The single most important default to change, when you are creating your master templates and layouts, are the text effects and the paragraph dialog.

Autofit is evil, so check the "Do Not Autofit" radio button. Usually, I prefer to have the text align in the top left corner, so I set the "Vertical Alignment" to top.

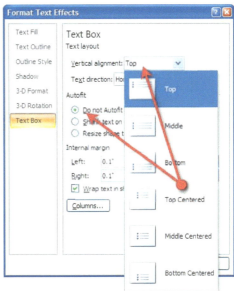

PARAGRAPH

Usually, I prefer to set the paragraph alignment to left. Line spacing needs to be entered. I start at a 0.8 multiple.

SLIDE TRANSITIONS

There are very rare exceptions to this practice. I set my slide transitions in PowerPoint to Fade at a medium or fast speed. In Keynote I use Dissolve at a half second.

TECHNIQUE
D'SLIDE

> Three rules of work:
>
> Out of clutter find simplicity.
>
> From discord find harmony.
>
> In the middle of difficulty lies opportunity.

Albert Einstein

THE VERY FIRST SLIDE

For the longest time I simply used my organization's logo as my first slide. But I learned something when watching other presentations. Logos are boring. And while the room settles in and introductions are being made, that first slide is on screen for a while.

So I started putting hooks on the first slide. For example, when I'm presenting on school safety to educators, I usually have something like this: "Revealing the Secret to Higher Test Scores."

For Carpe Audience Presentations I use the slide above. The point is that I want my audience curious and motivated to listen to more.

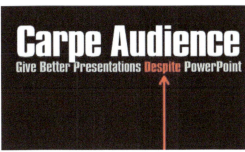

DECONSTRUCTION

The toughest thing about the Carpe Way is unlearning old habits and discarding incorrect practices. Certainly, the toughest practice to lose is the habit of bullet lists. So, the following pages show some examples of how to increase communication and decrease clutter.

" If you must use bullet lists, use them in your presenter notes. **Not on screen**."

THE POWER LIST: "KILL THE BULLETS"

If you must use bullet lists, use them in your presenter notes. Not on screen. Although my preference is to actually write out paragraphs, bullet lists aren't bad as prompts to keep you on target with your presentation and message. But not on screen.

Rather than a bullet list, take a look at the examples shown on the following pages. You can see where a few more more slides actually focus the audience on the data point. It's also much more effective visually and it allows you to build syncopation into your cadence.

The power list is the onscreen evolution of the bullet list. There are rules. No more than 7 words on the slide. The power list has a few formats. The general conversation with shared common elements. Or the individual point conversation, with each element unique to a slide. The power list demands attention. Both from the audience and the presenter.

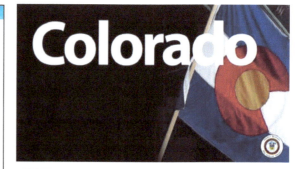

Risk Factors

- Substance Abuse
  - Nationwide, Colorado ranks:
    - 1st in marijuana use
    - 2nd in alcohol abuse
    - 15th in drug abuse
  - Colorado is 48th on spending for prevention and treatment
  - If a child starts drinking before the age of 15, they have a 40% chance of being an alcoholic
  - 5 million high schoolers binge drink at least once a month
  - Over 4 million youth (16% of 12 to 17 year olds) used marijuana in the last year
    - In Colorado, 30% reported marijuana use
- Mental Illness
  - 16% of DOC has serious mental illness
  - 50% to 75% of incarcerated youth have mental health disorders
    - Only around 50% have received treatment
  - Up to 19% of youth involved in CJS may be suicidal
  - Over 50% have co-occurring substance abuse

POWER LIST: "STATISTICAL SERIES"

What you see on this page is an example of how to restructure the slides to cover a series of numbers. On the upper left is an actual slide given at an actual presentation. The presenter gave a pretty good presentation, but the slides detracted from the outcome. This slide simply sucks. Some of the information on the slide is covered conversationally, but the bottom line is that just by projecting it, bad, bad cognitive overload has happened.

The conversation is about national ranking of teen substance abuse per capita. The dialog is simple:

Let's talk about Colorado.

Colorado ranks first, nationally, in teen marijuana abuse.

Second nationally in teen alcohol abuse.

15th in other teen drug abuse.

And Colorado is 48th nationally in prevention and treatment spending.

Might be a relationship there, let's talk about some more stats.

Replacing the slide above with the slides on the right did a few things. The main points about the depth of abuse could be sequenced quite quickly with the conversation. The images reinforced the abuse type. And with spending numbers (48th) the sequence could slow down, giving the presenter a transition into some of the other stats. One other technique could be achieved... Visual syncopation.

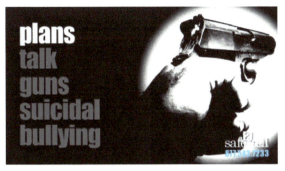

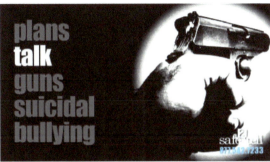

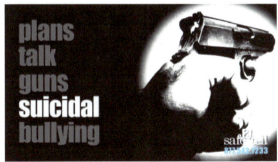

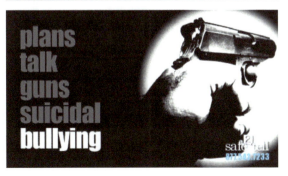

THE POWER LIST: "COMMON ELEMENTS"

In this presentation the conversation touches on a study done by the Secret Service regarding school attackers. The slide above is the original from the presentation. The slides on left replaced that single slide.

I call this the Common Element Power List. By taking the group of common elements and identifying each element with a single word, the relationship is maintained. Sequencing through the highlighted words, as the conversation continues allows each topic to gain focus, while still keeping the relationship between elements.

If you look at the slide above, you may notice that some things got combined, and others went away. For instance, during development, the story was slightly rearranged to separate "Warning Signs" into the next segment of the story.

"

What the Secret Service discovered about school attackers was that there was no consistent, reliable profile. But, in a lot of cases, these traits were common.

First Attackers make plans.

And they talk about them. In person and online. And they get encouraged by others.

Easy access to guns is another trait.

School Attackers are often suicidal.

And bullying is also a factor, with the Attacker either being a bully or having been bullied.

"

> ## How to avoid audience lunch loss
>
> - Don't use bullet lists
> - Don't use any clip art
> - Don't use complicated graphs
> - Don't use handshake pictures

THE POWER LIST: "ISOLATED INFO"

Here are some more examples of how to structure a Power List.

These slides are from the Carpe Audience presentation. You can see that the content of what would have been a traditional, no more than six words/six line, list has been restructured into individual slides. Slides that can be sequenced pretty quickly. Through isolation and images the interest is caught, the attention is kept, and the retention is increased.

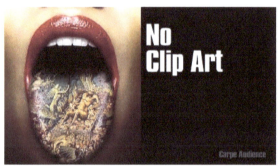

> **"** Sometimes I watch the audience **just as much** as I watch the presenter.**"**

A couple of things. I certainly couldn't have made this a traditional bullet list slide because the first bullet would have been incongruous, if not downright silly. The other thing is this: Really! No handshake pictures. They are so overused, so artificial, so just plain dumb, that you gotta stop using them. I've seen a lot of presentations. Sometimes I watch the audience just as much as I watch the presenter. I've seen folks in the audience visibly wince, cringe and recoil, when the handshake picture gets thrown.

This is another slide series where visual syncopation occurs. The rapid fire delivery of both the visual "No's" and the verbal delivery combine for a fast, effective communication. And when I stop to chastise handshake pictures... well it seems to just work.

Bullying

▸ Colorado Trust Major Findings
- **46% of young people have been hit, shoved, kicked or tripped at least once in the past month**
- **8% have been forced to do sexual acts at least once in the past month**
- 31% of those who have been attacked with a weapon at least once **attack others** – compared with only 2%who have not had this experience
- 29% of Colorado kids say they have bullied someone else at least once (compared to 23% of youth nationally)

THE POWER LIST: "HIGHLIGHT THE FACT"

These slides are from a presentation that includes information on bullying research. The purported strength of bullet lists is that conceptual grouping can be presented. But most bullet lists go downhill from there. (See above.)

This Power List example shows conceptual grouping in a format similar to the "Common Element" list shown previously. In the context of bullying, these four concepts are going to be discussed. Then, as the slides advance each concept is highlighted, while the group is still present, and the specific data associated with each concept is brought into detail.

Each concept is a story. Each data point is a story. Each story may have a statistical part and an example, bringing the statistic from the brain to the heart (emotion, remember emotion). When I present this type of Power List, I always end the story of the statistic, and the emotional anecdote, with a repetition of the stat itself.

" Increase retention and **retain** attention."

Remember "Say nothing without a purpose?" This style of presentation and slide construction, combined with deliberate, specific, single point delivery, will increase retention and retain attention.

There's one more side effect of this approach. It really forces you to look at the data and isolate the relevant from the fluff.

IMAGE SURFING

Not everybody trusts paintings but people believe photographs.

Ansel Adams

PICTURES

No clip art. That's the rule. But you need pictures. Compelling pictures that support your story of the moment. I use a number of sites to get photos at little or no cost.

http://sxc.hu - Stock Exchange
http://morguefile.com - Morgue File
http://commons.wikimedia.org - WikiMedia
http://flickr.com - Flickr
http://images.google.com - Google

With Flickr and Google you need to pay attention to whether or not you can use the image, but they are great for free association image surfing.

FREE ASSOCIATION IMAGE SURFING TECHNIQUE

One of the techniques I use to find pictures is image surfing. I usually start with Google, although Flickr is on the list too. With napkins in hand, I'll type in the key word written on my the napkin, like "Mona Lisa," and look at what comes up. From there, an image may spark something, like adding "Graffiti" to the search, then "Graffiti Face." You get the idea. One more trick with Google is when you highlight an image, often, a "Similar" link is visible. Click it.

NO MORE THAN THREE MINUTES.

There's a catch. No more than three minutes. If you haven't found something inspiring then it's time for tactic two. That's when I go to a site like Flickr or Stock Exchange and I start over. But this time, as I find an image that interests me, I'll click on the photographer's gallery to see their other work. Hopefully, other images might trigger an insight into what I should use as a visual to support the story.

COPYRIGHTS, USAGE AND SHYNESS

Pay attention to usage restrictions. But don't be shy about asking. A quick email to the artist or photographer might just yield a yes. (The images for the Trick Photography and Learn Multimedia Learning sections happened just that way.) And Flickr for instance has an advanced search option that filters by "Creative Commons" licensing.

THE GRID

SO SIMPLE IT MUST BE A TRICK

Not always the answer, but often it's good enough. The Grid is a composition trick that may make your slide layout a little more interesting. Here's how it works. It starts by dividing your screen into thirds, both horizontally and vertically. I do it with guidelines.

The intersections are your focal points. This is where you want to move the focal point of your type or photo. Compare the images below. One essential tip: Make sure the picture is bigger than the slide.

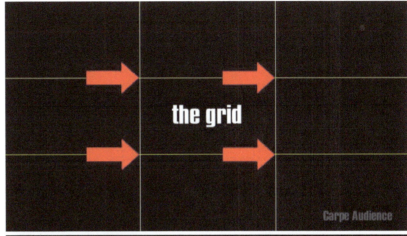

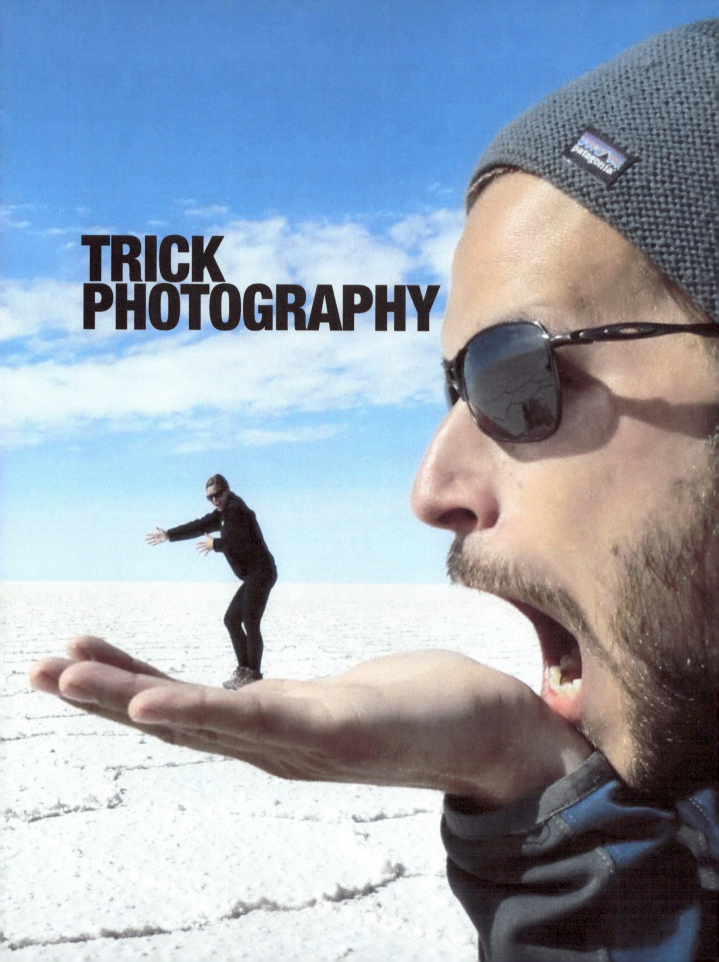

TRICK
PHOTOGRAPHY

The trick is in what one emphasizes. We either make ourselves miserable, or we make ourselves happy. The amount of work is the same.

Carlos Castaneda

PHOTOGRAPHY TRICKS

"People learn more deeply from words and pictures than from words alone." So you use pictures. Plenty of them. It used to be hard finding quality images at a reasonable cost. Even your own snapshots involved a trip to the local photo lab.

We live in amazing times. The digital camera and the internet give us a plethora of quality images at little or no cost. And it's immediate. Most of the photos in this book, and in every presentation I make, were found online or in my own photo collection, mostly free. (Teach by example.)

Since we're using lots of pictures, it's worth going over a couple more suggestions about presenting them.

" Don't **ever** do montages."

NO MONTAGES. NO! NONE

Lots of pictures, but not all on the same slide. Don't ever do montages. I'm going to say that again. Don't ever do montages. Just like too much text, too many pictures on the same slide will induce cognitive overload. When you have two or three or, heaven forbid, seven photos on the same slide, your audience starts looking for a seat on the bus to the beach. You've overloaded working memory and asked your audience's brains to process more than the buffer can hold.

Keep it simple. One picture at a time. (Alright, the exception is when I use a "Contact Sheet" graphic treatment.)

CROP OR BLEED

Where possible I prefer full screen, bleed off the edge, images. One image supporting your conversation at the time. Sometimes I use a split screen method. Picture on one side. Large type on the other. This technique actually forces composition into the grid, naturally.

Rarely, I crop the picture into a little box on screen. And the only time I do it, it's because of technical reasons. Usually insufficient resolution of the source image.

RESOLUTION

That takes us to resolution. How many pixels wide by how many pixels tall. If you're developing your presentation using an HD format, like 1280 x 720 then, at a bare minimum, your images need to be at least 1280 pixels wide. And hope the composition is on grid. Otherwise, you need more pixels. Why? So you can move the composition into the grid. Stock photo sites usually provide resolution information somewhere on the page. Google lets you define size in the Advanced Search dialog. Pay attention to this. Nothing is worse than the "jaggies" on screen.

If you need to adjust and crop your image, then make sure your image is larger than your slide. And if your source images just don't have the necessary resolution, then crop them to little squares or rectangles on your slide. But only as a very, very, very last resort.

FADE TO BLACK

While some images are shot on a black background, sometimes you need introduce a fade to black to isolate the image. While there aren't a lot of PowerPoint tutorials in this book, this is quick "How to" on creating this effect within either PowerPoint or Keynote.

STEP 1

Place your image and use the Grid.

STEP 2

Place a rectangle object on top of your image.

STEP 3

Give your rectangle object an advanced gradient. I selected the radial gradient. Here's the sorcery...

Make both the start and the end colors black. Then set the color in the center of your gradient to 0% Opacity. (Or for PowerPoint 100% Transparency)

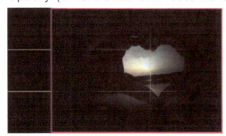

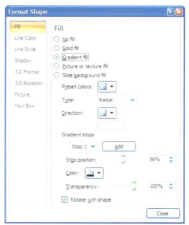

I want it painted black.

Rolling Stones

STEP 4

Adjust the size of the rectangle object. You may need to make it much bigger than the slide.

You may also need to remove extra color points on the gradient sliders.

STEP 5

Place your type.

STEP 6

This is the Appreciation part of the workflow.

MORE IMAGES. START OUT WITH ONE

Images change the entire tenor of your presentation. Remember this slide? This was the title slide of an earlier example.

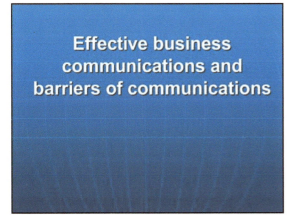

IMAGE SURFING

The reality is that this slide is far away from the Carpe Way. Let's start by changing the aspect ratio and going HD. Next a little Image Surfing, searching for the word "barrier." In less than two minutes I went from barrier, to wall, to the biggest wall on the planet. The Great Wall of China. Cropped and placed using the Grid.

CALL TO ACTION/GUERILLA TYPOGRAPHY

Finally, I retooled the title to be a call to action and I used the Grid and Guerilla Typography to place and tighten the text.

ADDING TYPE

Often an image can stand on it's own. You bring the story to life through the spoken word. Sometimes, it may be better to put type on screen. Either way, images are essential.

If you are superimposing text on an image, there is one other consideration about text... Color. Sometimes the color of your type (black or white, right?) is too close to the background. So adding a shadow or glow might be the way to pop the type off the image. The trick is to keep it subtle and keep it blurry. The default hard shadow in PowerPoint is icky. You want a soft shadow.

In Keynote it's easy to find the Graphic Inspector and adjust shadows. In PowerPoint, you need to go to the Format tab in the ribbon, select Text Effects, then Shadow. At the bottom of the drop down is "Shadow Effects." Be sure to set your shadow color to white if your type is black, and your background dark.

ANAMORPHIC SCALING

Squishy. That's where the height of the image is scaled differently than the width. Technically, it's called "Anamorphic Scaling," and it makes your pictures look squished. In PowerPoint, right click the image and select "Size and Position." Make sure that your height and width are the same percentage.

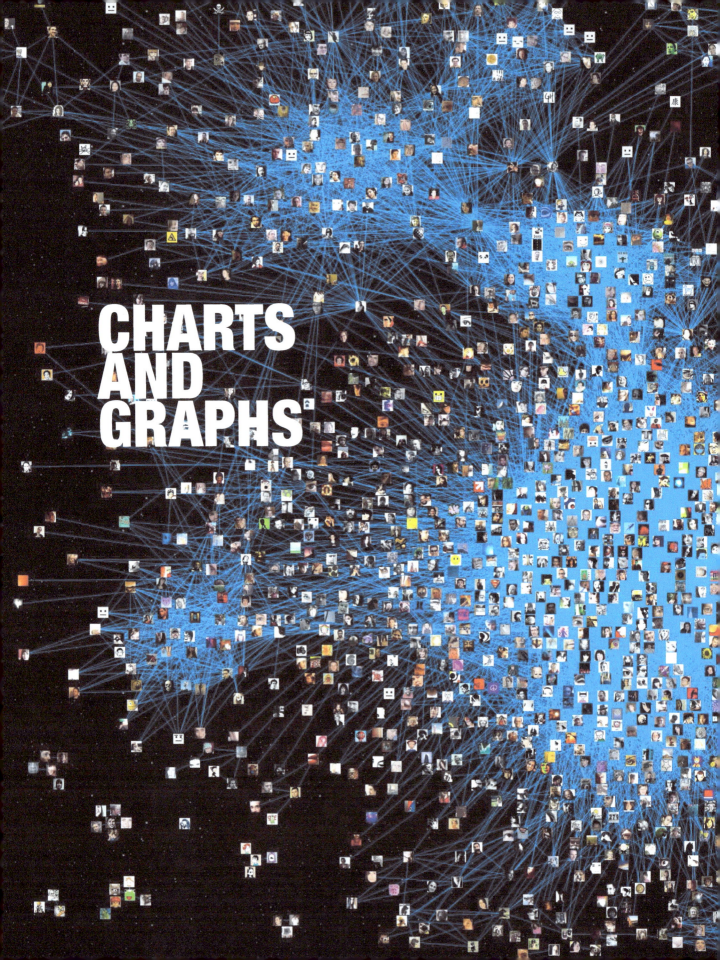

CHARTS
AND
GRAPHS

There are three
kinds of lies:
lies, damned lies,
and statistics.

Mark Twain

GRAPHS ARE THE LAST RESORT. UNLESS THEY'RE THE FIRST

This is a weird thing. Done well and done in context, graphs are a compelling ingredient in any presentation. That catch is "done well and in context." And it's hard to do graphs well. It's hard to understand the right context. Part of the problem is about the extreme ease of creating a jillion data points in the graphing sub-application of PowerPoint or Keynote. Another part is our own failure to identify the "call to action" prior to presenting the data. And finally doing graphs well is an arcane combination of both art and skill.

If you do graphs now and then, but data visualization isn't a big part of your presentation, this chapter is a surface level collection of tips and pointers.

If you need to really delve deep into data visualization, it's kinda like public speaking. There are a jillion books and resources out there. One of my favorite authorities is Stephen Few. His Perceptual Edge website (http://www.perceptualedge.com/) has a ton of resources available. Books, articles, white papers, samples, examples. A lot of it is available for downloading at no cost.

FINDING THE POINT

The first challenge with charts and graphs is identifying what the point of the chart or graph really is. Are you showing a trend. Or a peak. Or a comparison. Or a summation. The bottom line is really about asking yourself what is the call to action for the chart or graph. What conclusion do you want your audience to arrive at when you present data in a chart or graph? What's the story?

One strategy is to look at a chart or graph as a binary talking point. This is good. Or... This is bad. Either one invokes a call to action. "Sales are down, we must increase marketing. Or revisit R&D. Or look at the next generation."

Perhaps the answer is "Sales are up, we must increase marketing. Revisit R&D. And look at the next generation."

Sorry. That was cynical. But it illustrates the real point. What is the call to action that you want to invoke from displaying the chart or graph?

One more question. Does it need to be a graph at all? Just because numbers or percentages are involved, doesn't mean it automatically should be a chart. Sometimes the number is more effective.

TMI - DETAIL IS FOR THE REPORT OR HANDOUT

Too much information. That's usually the issue with most of the charts or graphs I've seen presented. Simple rule: If it's projected, less data, more point. The detailed chart or graph is in your handout or report. You know, on paper.

Seth Godin[15] suggests these three laws for chart design:

1. One Story
2. No Bar Charts
3. Motion

"One Story" is an easy one. Keep your story to one point, with a known conversational outcome. "No Bar Charts" is a little more difficult. Although

Godin makes the point that often bar charts are used when pie charts should be, there are times when a bar chart just makes the case. Stacked bar charts, though, should be handled like rattlesnakes. Unless you can bag it, you'll get bit.

Perhaps anytime you make a bar chart, you switch it to pie chart, or a line chart just to make sure the info you're presenting is relevant.

Motion is the last rule. Godin suggests creating two slides. "The first one shows where the data used to be, the second one, on the same axes, shows where it is or where it's going. Motion."

"Establish the first slide. Make your point about your source and its validity. Then press the advance button. Boom."

CHARTOHOLICS SHOUT DISAPPROVAL

When Godin posted his Three Laws, a number of folks chimed in from a data visualization perspective. Perhaps the biggest point of heartburn was the ban on bar charts.

One "Motion" technique I use, when I'm talking in "pie chart," is making several slides. Starting with what I'm going to talk about, get to the "Point" number, fill in the rest and end with my close. "Seventy Percent. We're pretty proud of that."

Some charting purists may object to my color selections, but after experimenting with a number of alternatives, this is what I ended up with. Hollywood.

The easy test for bar charts versus pie charts is whether or not the values add up to 100%. If they don't, your pie chart will be misleading.

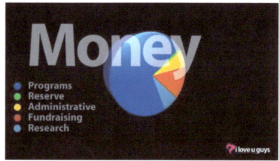

In this example, you can see that the pie chart on the right shows the values to better effect than the bar chart on the left.

Compare this example, to the next page. A line chart displays the trend more accurately.

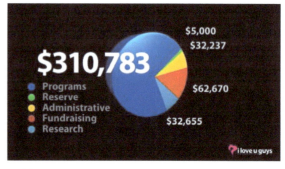

The slide examples on the next page shows types of interventions for a Colorado based anonymous tip line. The close is the number of tips received over the last 5 years.

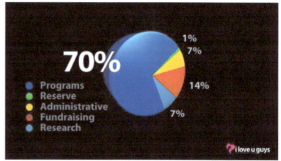

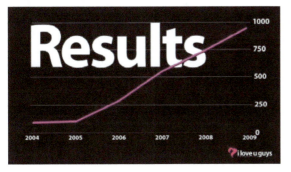

Type	Example	Encoding Method	
Value Comparison	Sales in different regions	Bars and Columns	
Ranking	Best selling products	Bars and Column	
Time-Series	Sales in the last 12 months	Lines to emphasize the overall trends or pattern	
		Points connected by lines to slightly emphasize individual values	
		Columns to emphasize and support comparisons between individual values	
Part-to-Whole	Market shares	Bars and Columns	
Deviation	Revenue Actual versus Budget in the last 12 months	Lines to emphasize the shape of the data	
		Points connected by lines to slightly emphasize individual data points	
		Bars and Columns to emphasize individual values	
Distribution	Support response times	Columns to emphasize individual values	
		Lines to emphasize the overall shape of the data	
Correlation	Relationship between employees heights in inches and their salary	Points and a trend line in the form of a scatter plot	

One of my charting faves, XLCubed (http://xlcubed.com/), publishes a blog, "More Information Per Pixel," that reveals their rules for creating effective charts.

USING MULTIMEDIA

Suddenly you're like a pirate, you're 65 years old and you've got an earring.

Fred Willard

HOW COOL IS THAT?

Adding audio or video to a presentation is an amazing feature. Embedding a media clip can bring emotion or a third person perspective or humor to the audience. The challenges with embedding media comes down to formats, size, quality and of course relevance.

I use news clips, videos, audio tracks, and home built multimedia. I make sure that the clips are sequenced into the Cadence of the presentation. And I battle the array of file formats in order to get the media into the presentation.

COLLATERAL DAMAGE IN THE BATTLES OF GIANTS

Wish it was simple. But it's not. Windows Media, Apple's Quicktime, Adobe Flash, WMV, MOV, FLV... it really has been a battle of the giants for the default format of online and desktop media. And users – you know, us – have been wounded in the process. There is no good answer. If you're using PowerPoint for Windows, then get everything converted to Windows Media. Keynote on the Mac, convert to Quicktime. Going both ways, well, it takes more work.

" Apple and Microsoft will collectively **punish me**."

Then there's the "Apple and Microsoft will collectively punish me," factor. Out of the box, Mac doesn't support WMV. PowerPoint on the Mac doesn't support WMV files, but it likes Quicktime. I do have a plugin for Quicktime on the Mac called Flip4Mac that lets me play WMV files, but not in PowerPoint for Mac. Until PowerPoint 2010 on Windows, PowerPoint wouldn't recognize Quicktime, even when you've installed the Quicktime application on your Windows machine.

It would be kind of funny if it wasn't so irritating.

Here's my current workflow when I am targeting PowerPoint for Windows. I build my presentations in Keynote on the Mac. For me, it's simply faster and more precise. I save all of my video as both Quicktime (MOV) and as Windows Media (WMV).

THE INTERNET WILL NOT EXIST AT YOUR NEXT GIG

Why not just link to media online? The answer is simple: Don't count on the internet working when you present. Even when I was demoing web-based software, I set up my laptop as a self contained web server and demoed right from my machine.

YOUTUBE RIPPING AND HOISTING THE JOLLY ROGER

The other challenge about copying media from online sites is that many of these sites would really prefer you don't. Even when the material isn't under copyright. As always, I suggest seeking permission to use media you find online. Copyright law is deep, arcane and confusing. I'm not a lawyer, but some aspects of "Fair Use" aren't that hard. Good luck matey.

THE MASHABLE LIST

Mashable had a pretty good list of online and local applications that can capture and convert media.

http://mashable.com/2007/05/05/download-youtube-video/

WEB BASED

Video Download X doesn't have a lot of options, but it's simple, and it works. It also enables you to share the YouTube video with your friends via e-mail. Unfortunately, all the files are called get_video, and you have to add the .flv extension manually.

http://videodownloadx.com

KeepVid is another simple site. No hassle, works not only for YouTube movies but for a number of other sites, including Google Video, MySpace Video, DailyMotion and others. Again, you have to add the .flv extension by hand.

http://keepvid.com

YouTube Downloads takes the cake in the longest domain name contest. It also separates itself by using a proxy for downloading videos, which means that you might be able to get videos even if YouTube access is blocked at your workplace or in the country you live. Just search Google for YouTube videos, and copy/paste the URL into YouTube Downloads.

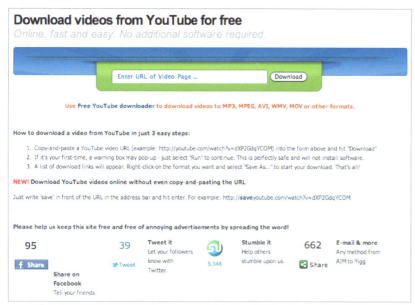

http://www.downloadandsaveyoutubevideos.info

YouTubia separates itself from the crowd by enabling you to search as well as download YouTube files. Options are scarce, but it works.

http://www.youtubia.com

VidGrab is another simple site that works with YouTube, Google Video, MySpace and Break.com. Besides the download function, the site also sports a top list of most viewed videos.

http://www.vidgrab.com

If Al Gore invented the Internet, I invented spell check.

Dan Quayle

> # Where there is a sea there will be pirates.

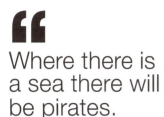

Greek Proverb

Vixy offers both downloading videos and converting them into DivX avi, mov, mp4, 3gp, or mp3 (for audio only) formats. The conversion works well enough, but sometimes results in slightly choppy playback.

http://vixy.net

Hey! Watch is an ambitious video encoding service with a large number of options, especially when it comes to converting videos to portable media player formats (it even supports my trusty iRiver H340.) Most online video converters often produce crappy results, with video and audio being out of sync, and this problem is also present on Hey! Watch, but it happens rarely.

http://heywatch.com

Zamzar is an online file format conversion site which can do a lot more than just converting YouTube videos to another format and downloading them to your hard drive, but it's doing a great job so we had to include it here. Thoroughly tested by us and highly recommended. See the video of it in action here.

http://www.zamzar.com

Media Converter can be a little slow, but the results of the video conversion are quite good. We've converted some YouTube videos to avi (mpeg4 + mp3) format and it worked well. The tool is not limited to video conversion; it also supports several audio and document formats.

http://www.mediaconverter.org

KcoolOnline is a web-based converter which supports 98 video sharing web sites, including YouTube. It has literally zero options, so it's recommended for those who like to keep it simple.

http://www.kcoolonline.com

Keep-tube is a free third party service that enables anyone to backup uncopywrited videos strictly for safety reasons. Just replace the word "you" with "keep-" in a YouTube url.

http://keep-tube.com

WINDOWS APPLICATIONS

VDownloader is a desktop application that catches YouTube, Google Video, and Grinvi video links from your clipboard. Start it up, copy the video URL and click download. It automatically converts the videos to mpeg or avi formats.

http:// www.softpedia.com/progDownload/VDownloader-Download-51327.html

YouTube Grabber downloads files from Youtube in .flv format. Copy and paste the URL of a video from YouTube into the program, press Grab, and the file will be downloaded into the same directory as the program.

www.download.com/Youtube-Grabber/3000-2071_4-10574801.html

Orbit Downloader is a desktop application which can download videos from a wide variety of sites. The download process is very simple, just hover your mouse over the video and you'll get a button that says Get It. The developers of the program claim that it's very fast (up to 500% faster, they say) due to its P2P download technology.

http://www.orbitdownloader.com

My Video Downloader. With all these free tools, it's actually funny to see a commercial one. It's called My Video Downloader, and while it does look solid and offers a lot of conversion options (a free trial which enables you to download 10 videos is available), we're not sure it offers enough to warrant a price tag.

http://myvideodownloader.com

KeepV is a desktop downloader as well as a converter, which converts the downloaded videos from flv to avi, mov, mp4, or 3gp formats.

http://keepv.com

VideoGet boasts being able to download video clips from more than 100 video sharing websites. We haven't tested all of them, so we're just going to take their word for it. It's a desktop application with a nice, simple interface and a solid number of options.

http://nuclear-coffee.com/php/products.php

TubeSucker is a desktop YouTube video downloader with some interesting options, including batch downloading large amounts of videos from a certain user. See the video tour on the site.

www.newrad.com/software/tubesucker/

> It has been said that Windows is the worst form of interface except all the others that have been tried.

Winston Churchill...
Or something like that.

It has been said that Macintosh is the worst form of interface except all the others that have been tried.

Winston Churchill...
Or something like that.

LINUX

Youtube-dl. Here's some love for Linux users. Youtube-dl is a program that lets you download YouTube clips in flv format, which both mplayer and VLC can easily chew up.

http:// www.nuxified.org/blog/download_youtube_video_files_with_youtube_dl

YouTube Ripper is not actually an application; it's a simple script that rips all videos that match a keyword, uploaded by a specific YouTube user. We don't really have ideas on what to use this for, but maybe you do! PHP port is also available.

http://nlindblad.org/2007/04/08/youtube-ripper-collectors-edition/

OS X

Perian is a bunch of open source utilities that enable Quicktime to play a large number of media formats.

http://perian.com

Get Tube is an OS X application which lets you download video or audio files from YouTube, DailyMotion and Kewego.

http://www.svcreation.fr/

PLUGINS

DownloadHelper is also a free Firefox extension for downloading and converting videos from many sites with minimum effort.

http://www.downloadhelper.net/

Vidtaker is a Firefox-only plugin that can download videos from most streaming websites: Google Video, YouTube, MySpace. It automatically converts the video to a DivX avi.

http://www.vidtaker.com

Ook? Video Ook! Yes, that's the full name of this Firefox plugin, which enables you to download videos from YouTube and several other video sharing web sites. It features one click downloading and integration with the popular DownThemAll Firefox plugin.

http://addons.mozilla.org/en-US/firefox/addon/2584

SLIDE HERDING

Rollin', rolling, rolling, though the streams are swollen, keep them doggies rolling. Rawhide.

Rain and wind and weather, hell-bent for leather, wishing my girl was by my side.

All the things I am missin', good vittles, love and kissing, are waiting at the end of my ride.

move 'em on,
head em up.

LET'S SADDLE UP POWERPOINT (OR KEYNOTE)

There you are. A string of stories ready to tell. Simple templates. Guerilla typography. Images and text falling into grids. Power Lists instead of bullet lists. Charts with purpose. How cool! Now it's assembly time. In the "Everything is a Story" chapter, you saw (and hopefully started) a cadence worksheet. Doesn't have to be fancy, just a spreadsheet with each of your stories and their associated run times.

Whether it's PowerPoint or Keynote, I prefer the Slide view versus the outline view, on the left. This option displays thumbnails of each slide. I also make sure that my Presenter Notes are visible.

One of the cool things about Keynote is the ability to group slides together. See how the three slides in the middle of the display on the left are indented. These are grouped and belong to the slide above. This behavior can sorta be accomplished in PowerPoint with the "Custom Show" feature. The point is, I can group and move slides depending on which presentation I might give to which audience.

PUT A STICKY NOTE ON YOUR MONITOR

Before you get too far, write down your call to action on a sticky note. Put it on your monitor.

COLLECT YOUR STORIES

I keep my text editor open behind Keynote. And all of my stories are open. I might print them out too. One story per page. Lets me shuffle things around if I need to. The point is to collect your stories so they are all together, ready for visual support.

You should also print out your Cadence Worksheet. You'll be noting times and types as you build your presentation.

ADDING PRESENTER NOTES

As you're building your slides, be sure to type (or copy and paste) your stories into the presenter notes. Whether it's talking points or complete sentences really depends on your style. But something must be written in the notes. You'll be presenting with sparse text or even just an image on screen. You're going to want your talking points visible for just you. Not to read from. But to remind.

You should also note the number of seconds it takes to tell that part of the story. Put the number at the bottom of your presenter notes, like this "Runtime: 20 Seconds." And fill out your Cadence Worksheet. You may have to tune your timings later, in order to achieve the cadence of the evening news.

STICK WITH YOUR TEMPLATES

You've already created your templates, so stick with them. If you paid attention, then you have simple templates with white type on a black background. Here's what's cool about that selection. It's simple. Let your images be your color. Not your type. If necessary, maybe add a shade of grey. (See Power Lists in the "Technique D'Slide" chapter.)

I can't stress enough the importance of this sparse design choice. By limiting your use of color to what exists already in pictures, you have accomplished two very important outcomes. First, it is visually more effective. Second, it removes the hassle, stress, and variability of messing around with color wheels.

LOOK AT YOUR NAPKINS

As you're producing your slides, look at your napkins, one story at a time. What one word, or short phrase did you write? Type it into your slide and move on. When you're done with that story, go back and look for your image opportunities. Go "Image Surfing" and place your pictures. It might turn out that your story has only one word or phrase on screen at a time. Or it may turn out that you need to sequence a series of images. Or text.

As you're placing images, remember, no montages and size your pictures so they fill the screen. Set your grid and move the focal point, if necessary. This will probably mean the picture is larger than the slide. No worries. Just verify that the resolution isn't too low. No jaggies.

Add a note about which slide is on screen, and the story type, in your Cadence Worksheet.

COLOR SELECTION

Almost every book on PowerPoint design includes a section on the color wheel and how to select and use complementary colors.

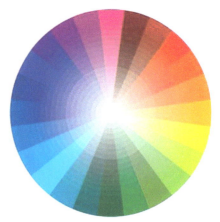

CONVENTIONAL COLOR WHEEL

You can purchase an analog color wheel at http://colorwheelco.com

THE CARPE COLOR WHEEL

Here's the Carpe Way. Color is for pictures. Otherwise use this.

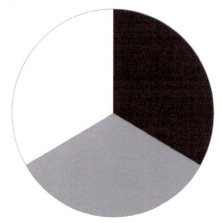

Time	Story	Type	Slide
0:00:10	Intro	Transition	Howdy
0:00:20			
0:00:30	Peace	Set the Stage	Peace
0:00:40			Images
0:00:50			Quote
0:01:00			
0:01:10			
0:01:20	About	Set the Stage	Not Easy
0:01:30			
0:01:40			
0:01:50			
0:02:00			
0:02:10			
0:02:20			
0:02:30			
0:02:40			
0:02:50			
0:03:00			
0:03:10			
0:03:20	Stand Up	Call to Action	Not Me
0:03:30			
0:03:40			
0:03:50	Legal Pad		
0:04:00			
0:04:10			
0:04:20			
0:04:30	Kids	Background	Not Said
0:04:40			
0:04:50			
0:05:00			
0:05:10			
0:05:20			
0:05:30			
0:05:40			
0:05:50	How Many	Transition	Zero
0:06:00			Hundreds
0:06:10	Media	Set the Stage	10 Years
0:06:20			
0:06:30			
0:06:40			
0:06:50			
0:07:00			
0:07:10			
0:07:20			
0:07:30			
0:07:40			
0:07:50			
0:08:00			
0:08:10			
0:08:20			
0:08:30			
0:08:40			
0:08:50			
0:09:00			
0:09:10			
0:09:20	Stats	Call to Action	300 Million
0:09:30	Safe2Tell	Call to Action	Can't Stop
0:09:40		Call to Action	Wrong
0:09:50		Background	Stats
0:10:00	Story	Background	9:23 AM

LOOK FOR VISUAL SYNCOPATION OPPORTUNITIES

As you're creating your slides, you may see opportunities to introduce some rapid fire changes. Seize them. Remember, you own the clicker. Here's an opportunity to use it.

How do you know? This may be a moment to review Aristotle's Rules of Rhetoric and the Rule of Three.

VERIFY REGISTRATION BETWEEN SLIDES

Make sure that your type size and position is exactly the same between slides. (Remember to turn off evil Auto-Fit.)

TRANSITIONS BETWEEN SLIDES

It is very, very rare, and only with purpose, that I do any fancy slide transitions. In PowerPoint I go to the slide sorter, select all of the slides and set the transition to "Fade" and the transition time to "Medium" sometimes "Fast." In Keynote same routine only the setting is "Dissolve" at about 0.5 seconds. No wipes. No pinwheels. Just a simple fade between slides. I think it's less jarring to your audience than the default straight cut between slides. Almost without exception, anything else is distracting. In fact, anymore, anything else smacks of amateur. Seriously.

ANIMATION ON THE SLIDE

The only time to add animation to a slide is when you are graphically illustrating movement in the physical world. Like a children's see-saw to illustrate the principle of the fulcrum.

Don't animate your text. Don't animate your Power List. Don't animate your logo. Do nothing without purpose. Just because PowerPoint lets you animate all of this stuff doesn't mean you should. Gratuitous animation adds absolutely nothing to your presentation and may actually distract your audience.

SEXY ANIMATED CURVY ARROWS

Don't. Really, just don't. I don't care what the Ninja[16] says.

INTERNET DEPENDENCY

Rely on internet access at your own peril. The grim reality is that no matter what your host says, the internet won't work during your presentation. So make sure you have all of your resources locally, in your presentation.

IT'S TIME TO MARCH

Let's revisit the Cadence Worksheet. I'm very serious about putting it together and keeping it maintained especially as a presentation evolves in time. I want the Longer, Less, Less, La, La La cadence happening every 10 minutes. I need to pay attention to the 10 Minute Barrier and make sure that I have a strong transition and a strong start to the next 10 minutes. And I don't leave it to chance, I time it. And document it. And tweak it.

This cadence is your secret weapon in delivering great presentations. If leverages the natural tendencies of human attention and audience conditioning. If you are slipping in your cadence, hopefully the Cadence Worksheet will help you see that in advance.

ESSENTIAL
IS
REHEARSAL

> In theory there is no difference between theory and practice.
>
> In practice there is.

Yogi Berra

PRACTICE MAKES PERFECT

If you take no other advice in this book, please take this advice. Practice. The single most effective way you can deliver better presentations is by practicing. You know, rehearsal. Now some folks think that practicing consists of sitting there and silently reading your speaker notes to yourself. Pshaw. That's for the airplane. Not rehearsal.

STAND UP. SPEAK OUT

What I'm talking about is setting your up your software in presenter view, standing up and delivering your presentation. Out loud. As if there was an audience on the other side of your monitor. If you've got it, plug in your projector or another monitor, so you can see what the audience sees too.

If you have a microphone, use it. And record your presentation. Walk around as you talk. Step past the imaginary stage and into the imaginary audience.

When you do this, something interesting will occur. You will find parts of your presentation where you just can't say it like you wrote it. (Hey, someone put marbles in your mouth!) Write it differently so you can say it better. Some of the slides may not work, so they need to be changed.

USE YOUR CLICKER

Use your clicker. Really. Even if you're standing right in front of your keyboard, and the arrow key is just a reach away, use your clicker instead. Get used to it. Own it.

IT'S REHEARSAL NOT MEMORIZATION

This is the hardest thing to convey. You should be practicing giving your presentation. Not memorizing it. Whether you wrote your stories out in presenter notes, or just outlined your talking points, you shouldn't be trying to deliver a word for word rendition every time.

Print out your Cadence Worksheet. If you broke your presentation down into a series of stories, then you are just telling a little story for this part of the presentation. A story you already know. A story you can tell again. Compare your delivery time for your stories to what you originally jotted down when you wrote it.

FIRST PASS

Your first pass will likely reveal some changes. Take the time to make those modifications. Then keep going. Get as many of these changes done that first time around.

TRY, TRY AGAIN

Once is not enough. You need to run through your presentation at least twice more, as if you were on stage. Beginning to end. Did you hit your time target? And if you have friends, family or roommates willing to help, then they are your first audience.

ADD 10%

One last observation. I've found that I consistently run 10% longer when I actually deliver my presentations in front of a live audience than when I rehearse. I now build that into my target times.

MASTER THE PRESENTER VIEW AND RULE THE WORLD

Pay no attention to that man behind the curtain.

The Wizard of Oz

WHAT YOU SEE IS WHAT YOU GET. OR NOT

This is one of those things that I thought was obvious. But in talking to people about their presentation delivery, an alarming majority had no idea that this capability even existed. You see, PowerPoint and Keynote have a very powerful feature. In PowerPoint it's called "Presenter View." In Keynote, "Presenter Display." Effectively, Presenter View let's you show your notes, the current and next slide(s), and elapsed time on your laptop monitor, while the projector shows just the slide.

Now if you have already used and mastered the Presenter View, then carry on. Nothing to see here. But if not, you absolutely must mess with this until you have it down pat.

In PowerPoint it lives in the Slide Show tab.

In Keynote, Presenter Display lives in Preferences.

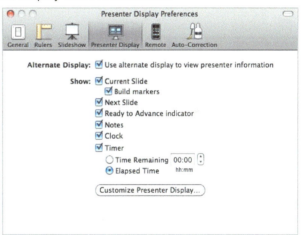

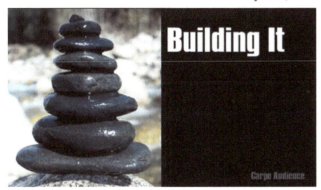

Here is the slide that is projected

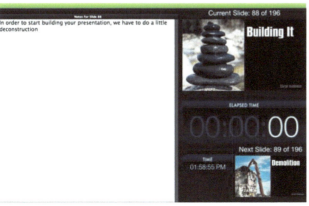

This is displayed on my laptop screen

THE CATCH

Here's why I think so many folks miss this feature. In PowerPoint, you have to have multiple displays active on the PC just to see what it even does. Multiple monitors on your desktop machine, or a projector or monitor plugged in on your laptop.

So try it. Plug in a second monitor or projector into your laptop. And mess around until you get what you need. At a bare minimum, master the settings so that you can set up an alien machine at the drop of a hat.

LIGHTS
CAMERA
CAMPFIRE

Yesterday is gone.

Tomorrow has not yet come.

We have only today.

Let us begin.

Mother Teresa

THE GIFTS

When you get to do a presentation you are given gifts. The gift of time. The gift of attention. The gift of space. The gift of the "Talking Stick." The people in the room have agreed to listen to you tell your stories. They have agreed to sit down and pay attention when you do it. They've agreed to turn off the ringers on their cell phones. The host has given you the gift of a projector and a sound system.

You should honor those gifts and seize the day.

" **Carpe** Diem."

Because that's what they are. Gifts. In fact, if you look at a typical room at a conference there's somewhere between 50 and a 1000 people in the room. Do the math. Just in employer overhead... wages, benefits and contributions, you're looking at least $40 an hour, per head. Add the cost of the room, maybe breakfast or lunch and you can figure that the gift you've been given is worth about $5,000 per hundred. Whether your audience is white collar professionals or blue-jeaned tradesmen, that number is about the same. (Students are cheaper, for the moment.)

Here's a personal example. I gave a presentation in New York City to a room jam-packed: about a thousand people. The host gave me two hours that morning. Do the math. There was over $100,000 in wages and overhead, that morning, sitting in that particular room. I did my damnedest to make it worth their time. In the end, they stood and clapped. Carpe Audience.

BUTTERFLIES? YOU'RE A ROCK STAR

I said earlier that there are a jillion books on public speaking. This ain't one of them. But maybe a couple of words might help. First of all, butterflies are normal. If you know in advance that you might get a little tingling in your tummy, then get ready to embrace it. How often do you get to have that feeling? My advice, Carpe Butterfly.

" You have a kick-ass slide deck and **you know how** to sling it."

Keep in mind, you aren't doing your presentation for the first time. You've rehearsed. And, if you followed the techniques described in this book you have a kick-ass slide deck and you know how to sling it. And the audience will be more attentive because you aren't putting them on a bus to the beach. None of that bad, bad cognitive overload for you. No sir.

You also broke your presentation down into little stories. Eating the elephant one bite at a time. You have a call to action, so you know what you want your audience to do when you're done with your presentation.

So, take a deep breath. You and your audience share a desire. They want you to give a great presentation. So do you. They even put your name in the program. Like a Rock Star.

SWAGGER? YOU'RE NOT REALLY A ROCK STAR

Confidence is good. But keep in mind that you are usually just a name on a program. Even when they stand and clap, don't let it go to your head. Just revel in the moment... You were given a gift. Appreciate the moment. Don't assume it's a right, or that it will happen every time you present. There is a balance. If a little swagger enters your walk, or your talk, take a deep breath and remember the gifts.

" Voila! The **fight or flight** response."

SWAGGERING BUTTERFLIES

Here's my theory. The butterflies and the swagger are really just the same thing. It's called the hypothalamus and inside this part of your brain, neurosecretory cells tell your pituitary to ramp up a chemical response while the hypothalamus simultaneously jolts out an electrical signal. Know fear. Or at the very least, the perception and acknowledgment of a threat. And there you have it. Voila! The fight or flight response. It's very real. It's very physiological. And it's very normal. But don't stress, you may be able to ratchet it down just a bit.

DAVID GROSSMAN AND DEEP BREATHS

Lieutenant Colonel, David Grossman[17] is a fascinating presenter. He doesn't use PowerPoint. He uses a handful of transparencies, a pair of easels with giant sticky notes and big fat markers.

During his presentations for Law Enforcement and Military, Lt., Col. Grossman demonstrates a breathing technique to combat stress. It goes like this:

Breathe in through your nose while counting one, two, three, four. Hold, two, three, four. Breathe out through your mouth, two, three, four. Wait, two, three, four.

Try it now:

> In through your nose, two, three, four.
> Hold two, three, four.
> Out through your mouth, two, three, four.
> Wait, two, three, four.

Do this a few times.

I use this technique prior to most presentations. Whether I've got too many butterflies or too much swagger. Maybe it sounds too simple to be true, but it works for me. If the butterflies are pesky, or the swagger is, give it a try. It may work for you too.

SCOUTING

One other secret is to scout the event. Online, through interviews and in person. This helps you understand your host. Your audience. And the venue. Prior to the event, I get some information from and about the host. It may be useful to bring some of this into the presentation. I also try to gauge the audience composition. Are they new to the topic, or seasoned veterans. A single profession or a mix of professions with a

When you get on stage, you can be anything. You are removed from reality in a way, the real world.

Suzanne Farrell

Nothing earth shattering has happened in men's fashion. How much can you do with men's clothes?

Calvin Klein

common concern. Older? Younger? A lot of this can be done online, or with a quick phone call to the host.

The other scouting mission is before the presentation. If you have a media rich presentation, then test your video and your audio. Test your clicker from around the room.

CLOTHES

I am probably not the right authority on fashion, but I will share my practices on keynotes and plenaries. I've been fortunate in that for my presentations a semi casual wardrobe is acceptable. But I always wear the same thing for these presentations. A freshly pressed, button down white dress shirt, black-black-black unfaded jeans and my favorite grayish sport jacket. Colors selected straight from the Carpe Audience Color Wheel. (Did I mention that I am probably not the right authority on fashion?)

I make it a point to wear the same thing for two reasons. First, I don't worry about changing my fashion statement. Second, if the presentation is video taped, the potential for using several different presentations in a single video compilation is greater.

Having said that, my advice is do what is either comfortable or appropriate. The nature of my presentation lets me be a little more casual. But if I thought it would be more effective, I would be in full, power tie, three piece, charcoal or black pinstripes.

" I take the lectern **off the stage**."

POCKETS

Unless you are doing magic or sleight of hand, empty your pockets. And keep your hands out of your pockets during the presentation. If either of these tips is unachievable, sew your pockets shut.

LECTERNS AND PODIUMS

If at all possible, I take the lectern off the podium or the stage. (Better yet, I ask someone else to.) I don't need the fortress in front of me. If the only mic is short wired to the podium, then I see if it's comfortable to stand beside it. (Remember you may have purchased a wireless microphone. Now might be the time to plug it in.)

Finally, if the host set it up so that it's nearly impossible not to stand behind the podium, then there you are. One quick word of advice. Try not to tap on the podium when you present. You're behind the podium because you need sound reinforcement for your voice. The podium microphone will sound like a drum when you grab the podium.

LAVALIERE MICROPHONES

Learn the switch. Turn it off. Here's why. You need to get into the habit of turning off the lavaliere microphone every time you step off stage. I'm going to say it again. Step off the stage, turn off the mic.

Here's why. Lavalieres have a remarkable sensitivity and range. Conversations in the hall, or the restroom, don't need to be in the PA.

LIGHTS

Some of my presentations have a lot of multimedia. News clips, image and music compilations and other types of video. When these are running it's better to have a darker room. But, when I'm talking, I want a slightly brighter room. Sometimes I have to take a medium. Sometimes, either the host or a colleague can dim and brighten the lights over the course of the presentation. But I never present in a dark room. The darkest I let it get is dusk. The campfire still has to shine on the tribesman with the "Talking Stick."

LEARN SILENCE

This is the hardest thing I ask you to learn. Silence. Ten seconds of silence can feel like an eternity. But silence is powerful. Whenever I use a quote, I say it while images are running. Then I present it in text and shut up. Body language is important. I turn to the screen and read the quote, silently in my mind. Then I turn back to the audience before I start speaking and advance the slide.

In other parts of some presentations, I use some powerful multimedia. For a couple of them, as the images and music fade to black. I pause. Not a word. Let the tension sizzle for just a bit longer.

LEARN TO SHOUT

Sometimes you may need to bring the volume up. Practice with your mic, and move the thing away. If you have lavaliere clipped on, tilt your head up. The point is that you already know how to shout. But shouting with a microphone can have disturbing outcomes, if you haven't practiced in advance.

LEARN TO WHISPER

You also may have the opportunity to whisper. Practice your stage whisper so that it can be heard. And where the mic needs to be.

> Saying nothing... sometimes says the most.

Emily Dickinson

" I've seen dozens of presentations where the presenter believed the **"Tell a Joke Rule,"** and bombed."

JOKES ARE FOR COMEDIANS

I don't do jokes very well. So I don't tell them. I can, occasionally, spin a phrase or reference that brings a chuckle. I've seen a couple of great presentations where the presenter litters their presentation with jokes. It works for them. I've also seen dozens of presentations where the presenter believed the "Tell a Joke Rule," and bombed. Usually within the first 60 seconds of their presentation. Uh Oh... I hear seagulls.

If you are good at telling jokes, don't be shy about telling a couple. But if not, don't. There are other ways to bring humor into your presentation.

> **What do you get when you cross a snowman with a vampire?**
>
> Frostbite.

WHERE HUMOR WORKS

The easiest way to bring humor into a presentation is through a picture. If you can find one in context, then use it.

You should avoid Lolcats though. http://icanhascheezburger.com/ Don't even go to the website. You'll get lost there for hours. Should also avoid http://walmartpeople.com.

TURN OFF SLEEP MODE, DISPLAY SLEEP AND HIBERNATION

PowerPoint or Keynote shouldn't go to sleep during the middle of a presentation. But if you scouted in advance, then you already set up the projector. If you haven't started your presentation, then your display or even the computer may go to sleep. Often this results in the computer "Losing" the projector. You don't want to be fussing with this while you're getting introduced. So set up a power setting that doesn't put the computer or display to sleep.

COUNT YOUR BLESSINGS THEN USE THEM

I have been blessed with a deep, resonant voice. It's a useful presentation tool. And I use it. I am pretty good at putting together little multimedia clips. So I do. Outside of being a few inches inches north of six feet, I'm pretty average in appearance. And my fashion sense, well remember the Carpe Color Wheel?

I've shared the stage with a presenter who is well spoken, six foot two and Hollywood gorgeous. And she has fashion sense. She leverages her blessings and looks fabulous in the spotlight. Just walking on stage, she achieves Medina's "You've only got seconds to get their attention." For her it works with men, women and children. I've seen presenters drop in an *a cappella* moment, sleight of hand magic tricks, even one who tap danced his rim-shots.

The point is this. Don't be afraid to bring your blessings to the table and use them.

INVENTORY YOUR CURSES AND OVERCOME THEM

I still occasionally drop an Ummm into the presentation. I'm getting better. Much better. It's because I recognize it and I attack it. I take the time to watch the video of my presentations. For a while I wore a rubber band on my wrist and snapped it, every time I said Ummm. (Not really. But I thought about it.)

Sometimes you're dealt a raw deal. If something can't be overcome, then see if you can make it iconic. The audience is hungry for stories, even if the story is a tough one.

CARPE AUDIENCE

Appreciate the gift and have a blast. You get to give a presentation. Yippee! That's how it feels to change the world.

"Yesterday is gone. Tomorrow has not yet come. We have only today. Let us begin." Carpe Audience.

Most executives, many scientists, and almost all business school graduates believe that if you analyze data, this will give you new ideas.

Unfortunately, this belief is totally wrong.

The mind can only see what it is prepared to see.

Edward de Bono

THE BOARDROOM

Whether it's a handful of executives, or a plethora of middle management or even the heckling marketing or IT department, boardroom presentations are different from the ballroom or the workshop. Usually you're there by invitation. Usually you're either updating or pitching. (Apologies in advance to Edward Tufte.[18]) And that's the first style differentiator. Updates, in a lot ways, are easier. Just the facts ma'am. Doesn't mean there isn't work involved. But it's directed and formulaic.

The pitch is a little more complex. Whether you're selling a project or strategy to your own company or a product or service to a prospect, ducks need to be toeing lines before you walk in the door.

THE UPDATE

The key to a successful update presentation is having a good written report. That is your handout. That's what you email. Never ever email your PowerPoint or Keynote presentation. If you're not there to give a presentation, the slides in situ are meaningless. You need a report. Full sentences. Paragraphs. Logical thought. You know, work.

Usually, you hand it out in advance. The presentation is no different than any other presentation prepared in the Carpe Way. A clear call to action. No bullet lists. No more than seven words per slide. Pictures. During your presentation, it's absolutely okay to reference pages or paragraphs in your written report.

THE PITCH

The pitch is probably a little different. Now, this isn't a book about sales development, that's a whole different animal. But whichever sales strategy you employ, you need flexibility to take your presentation whatever direction your audience wants to travel. That means you need the ability to vary the detail based on audience need.

HYPERLINKING IS THE ANSWER. WHAT'S THE QUESTION?

To accomplish this seamlessly demands a little more work – hyperlinks. In PowerPoint, I wish it was as simple as adding hyperlinks to your text. But it's not. Clearly, the discovery of hyperlinks got the Microsoft folks very enthusiastic about colors and underlines acting as visual indicators. Not to be outdone by the animation team, the PowerPoint hyperlink development team jumped on the visual cue bandwagon and deemed that any hyperlink that was text must have an underline. And will. Can't get rid of it. Really. (Shouted curses are not only an acceptable part of the workflow in PowerPoint, but occasionally mandatory.)

In Keynote, it's a preference in Auto-Correction. Uncheck "Underline text hyperlinks on creation." But in PowerPoint creating hyperlinks without underlines means putting your text in shapes or putting transparent shapes

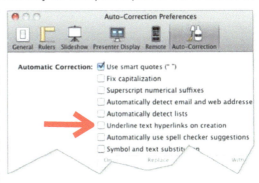

over your text. It's the shape that you define as the hyperlink. And that's the trick in Power-Point. So, it means a little more work to build your presentation. By the way, if you're using an ancient version, the transparent shape trick doesn't work. You're just stuck putting text in shapes and losing the fill. Did I mention cursing?

MAKE IT SO

After my stories are done, and my napkins waxed, I start building my slides pretty much like any other presentation. One slide at a time. One difference though...

Often I'll have a Power List right up front. Beyond outlining what I'm going to talk about, it's also a menu with hyperlinks to my main points.

In my interior slides I set up a master that has the logo link back to the Power List slide.

WORK IT BABY. WORK IT

It's all in the delivery. Unlike a campfire, where your laptop is over by the kindling and you're clicking away with your clicker, in the boardroom I try to use a wireless mouse. Call me old school, but the trackpad just isn't the same. I need to track and click in the hyperlink zones

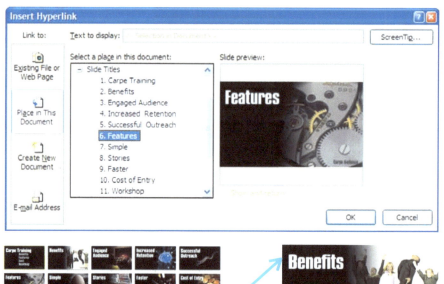

quickly when I'm in linking to my main points. Or when I click the logo to get back to the Power List. I can also proceed with the next slide with just a left click on the mouse. Sometimes holding the mouse just like a clicker.

Mastering "Presenter View" is knowing when not to use it. If there is any chance that anyone but me can see my laptop, I mirror displays with the projector. No reading ahead. With the hyperlinked slide deck you can dive deep or just skim. It depends on the room. The benefit is flexibility. But if you thought the clicker carried challenges, then this style needs much more practice.

The illustration on the right shows the link map. A normal click advances to the next slide. A hyperlink brings things back.

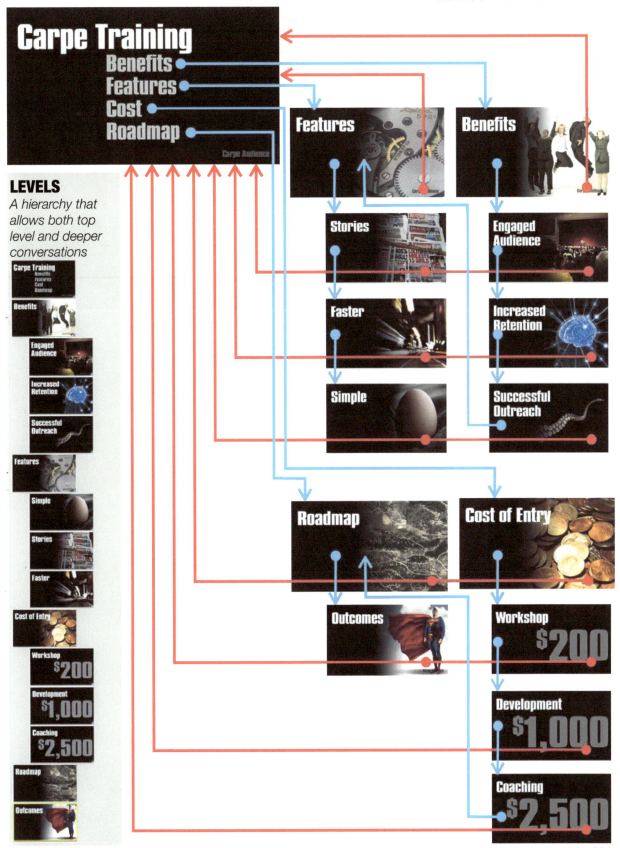

THE
HISTORIE
OF
FOVRE-FOOTED
HANDOUT THEORY

Defcribing the true and liuely figure of euery Beaft, with a difcourfe
of their feuerall Names, Conditions, Kindes, Vertues (both naturall and
medicinall) Countries of their breed, their loue and hate to Mankinde, and the
wonderfull worke of God in their Creation, Prefervation,
and Deftruction.

Ᵹary for all Diuines and Students, becaufe the ftory of euery Beaft is amplified with Narrations out of Scrip-
tures, Fathers, Phylofophers, Phyfitians, and Poets : wherein are declared diuers Hyerogliphicks, Emblems,
Epigrams, and other good Hiftories, Collected out of all the Volumes of CONRADVS GESNER, and all
other Writers to this prefent day.   By EDWARD TOPSELL.

The   Gorgon

LONDON,
Printed by William Iaggard.
1607.

> Think
> twice
> before
> burdening
> a friend
> with a
> secret.

Marlena Dietrich

WHEN YOU GO TO A MOVIE, DO YOU BRING THE SCRIPT?

In PowerPoint lore, printing little pictures of your slides comprises what is called a handout. This practice is another one of those curly DNA hooks that really defies the notion of a great presentation. You see, with a handout that is little pictures of your bullet lists, you are just adding one more bank of visual noise in your balance of signal to noise ratio. You're letting the audience read ahead. No more surprise. You afford them the opportunity to stop looking and listening to you. (Do I smell the ocean?)

There's more. At about three slides into your presentation, seasoned PowerPoint viewers will thumb to the back of your handout and begin to wager amongst themselves on the final runtime of your presentation. Occasional side bets on time 'til "In Summary..." OhThankGoditsOver.

On the other hand, there are studies indicating that when people write, on paper, while they are learning, retention increases. Hence, handouts.

WHY NOT ASK WHAT THEY DO WITH THEIR HANDOUTS?

I decided to tackle this conundrum a different way. I asked people what they wrote on their handouts. Both in business and at conferences, some of what I found was predictable. For instance, contact information and web addresses top the list. I also saw something else. A lot of people wrote "Action Items" on their handouts. Something said during the presentation triggered a "To do." Hardly ever did someone write on the little lines next to every slide. (There's an exception for students. Often they call their handout scribbles, "Class Notes".)

The bottom line is I produce a very different handout than the "Print Handouts" from PowerPoint. I start with a cover page that talks about the presentation and the handout. Next, I provide a notes section that generally follows the presentation. Then I provide a questions page so folks can jot questions down as they occur. I list every resource cited in the presentation. I usually have an evaluation. The last page is an info sheet on the program.

For you it might be a brochure or a data sheet or your report. Here is an opportunity to put structured information into the hands of your audience. Sometimes it's ready for pickup at the end of the presentation, not in advance, Sometimes it's the last page.

THE OTHER HANDOUT

That's all fine and good for the ballroom or for workshops. But there is another type of handout. The report. Often in business, or institution, PowerPoint has become the medium for updates, reports, assessments and such. I already said that PowerPoint is not a word processor or desktop publishing application. Yet, here we go again.

I think the answer is really this. When you're asked to do a "Report" in PowerPoint, don't. Write your report in a decent word processor. Use complete sentences. This written report is your "Handout." Your presentation now has a few calls to action. One is to read the report. Another is to highlight your conclusions, research or updates. Don't ever email your PowerPoint to someone. Email a report. Or a summary. Without you to present it, your PowerPoint is meaningless.

HANDOUT 1

EVENT:
Information Session, House Education Committee

DATE:
01/17/2011

PRESENTATION:
Learning how Colorado is teaching the nation about school safety.

PRESENTED BY:
John-Michael Keyes
Executive Director
The "I Love U Guys" Foundation

Email: johnmichael@iloveuguys.org
Service: 303.426.3100
Home Office: 303.838.1188
Cell: 720.289.1964
Post: Box 1230 - Bailey, CO 80421

ABOUT THIS PRESENTATION:
This presentation was developed using the Carpe Audience Practice, a scientific approach to presentation development and delivery. What this means is that it may not be necessary to take notes during the presentation. Rather, sit back and enjoy the moment. You'll learn tons simply by watching and listening. But, if you do use note-taking as a learning device, there is room in this handout to take notes.

ABOUT THIS HANDOUT:
This handout has three sections: Notes, Questions and Resources

The Notes section follows the main topics covered in the presentation. The page displays two columns, one for notes and one for personal action items that might result during the presentation.

If you have questions during the presentation, please jot them down on the Questions page and these can be answered after the presentation.

The Resources page includes information on resource material presented.

THANK YOU FOR YOUR TIME:
You have given me a gift – your time. It is my intent to provide value for your gift. If at any time you decide that your time can be better spent elsewhere, don't be shy about leaving. Seriously. But, while you're here, turn the ringers off of your cell phone and if you need to take a call, please step out. - *John-Michael*

NOTES

NOT SAID _____

_____

_____

NOT ME_____

_____

_____

NOT HERE_____

_____

_____

PCHS_____

_____

_____

WHAT WE LEARNED _____

_____

_____

GOVERNMENT ACTIONS _____

_____

_____

NIMS - NATIONAL INCIDENT MANAGEMENT SYSTEM (SEE RESOURCE PAGE FOR TRAINING LINKS)

_____

_____

THE STANDARD RESPONSE PROTOCOL

Lockout - Secure the Perimeter
Lockdown - Locks, Lights out of Sight
Evacuate - To a Location
Shelter - (Name the hazard, provide a method. ie: "Shelter for Tornado - Drop cover and hold.")

_____

_____

PLAN WINS_____

_____

_____

ACTION ITEMS

_____
_____
_____
_____
_____
_____
_____
_____
_____
_____
_____
_____
_____
_____
_____
_____
_____
_____
_____
_____
_____
_____
_____
_____
_____
_____
_____
_____
_____
_____
_____

QUESTIONS

3

TOPIC:_____

_____

_____

_____

_____

TOPIC:_____

_____

_____

_____

_____

TOPIC:_____

_____

_____

_____

_____

TOPIC:_____

_____

_____

_____

_____

TOPIC:_____

_____

_____

_____

_____

TOPIC:_____

_____

_____

_____

_____

ACTION ITEMS

RESOURCES

4

THE "I LOVE U GUYS" FOUNDATION

Mission:
To restore and protect the joy of youth through educational programs and positive actions in collaboration with families, schools, communities, organizations and government entities.
Web: http://iloveuguys.org
Service: 303.426.3100

The Standard Response Protocol
All materials are available at no charge to public K-12 at:
http://iloveuguys.org/srp.html

Safe2Tell
Web: http://safe2tell.org
Phone: 719.520.7435

FEMA Training
Web: http://training.fema.org

Suggested NIMS Courses
IS-100.SCa - Introduction to ICS
IS-200 - ICS for Single Resources
IS-300 - Intermediate ICS Training
IS-362 - Emergency Planning for Schools
IS-700.a - NIMS, An Introduction
IS-800.b - National Response Framework

Colorado Attorney General's Office
Interagency Cooperation Template
Web: http://coloradoattorneygeneral.gov/initiatives/
youth_violence_prevention/interagency_cooperation

Center for the Study and Prevention of Violence
School Climate Survey
Web: http://colorado.edu/cspv/
Phone: 303.492.1032

Colorado Senate Bill 181
http://www.leg.state.co.us/clics/clics2008a/csl.nsf/fsbillcont3/F8FCF1B1
742ABEBA872573680052EE58?open&file=181_enr.pdf (or search for
181 here: http://www.leg.state.co.us/clics/clics2008a/csl.nsf/)

Summary Report Colorado Bureau of Investigation
Web: http://extras.mnginteractive.com/live/media/site36/2007/0327/
20070327_023001_CBI%20Case%20Report.pdf

Presentation Reference
This presentation was prepared using Carpe Audience Practices. Find
out more: Web: http://carpeaudience.com

Peace
It does not mean to be in a place where there is no noise, trouble, or
hard work.

It means to be in the midst of those things and still be calm in your heart.

CARPEAUDIENCE

EVALUATION

5

My Role:
- ☐ Teacher
- ☐ Administrator
- ☐ School Resource Officer
- ☐ Other Law Enforcement
- ☐ Federal/State/Local Gov't
- ☐ Emergency Manager
- ☐ Other _____

My Organization:
- ☐ School
- ☐ District
- ☐ Department
- ☐ Agency
- ☐ School Board
- ☐ Private Sector
- ☐ Other _____

Number of Students:
- ☐ N/A
- ☐ 1 - 100
- ☐ 101 - 500
- ☐ 501 - 5000
- ☐ 5001 - 25000
- ☐ 25001 - 50,000
- ☐ Other _____

Rate the following from 1 to 4 where 1 is strongly disagree and 4 is strongly agree.
Presentation Organization:

Presenter 1 Presenter 2 Presenter 3 Presenter 4

1 2 3 4	1 2 3 4	1 2 3 4	1 2 3 4	My interest was quickly engaged.
1 2 3 4	1 2 3 4	1 2 3 4	1 2 3 4	I could easily follow the main points..
1 2 3 4	1 2 3 4	1 2 3 4	1 2 3 4	Points were presented in a logical order.
1 2 3 4	1 2 3 4	1 2 3 4	1 2 3 4	Each subject presented was relevant.

Presentation Content:

1 2 3 4	1 2 3 4	1 2 3 4	1 2 3 4	The points made were well supported.
1 2 3 4	1 2 3 4	1 2 3 4	1 2 3 4	I was convinced by the speaker's presentation.
1 2 3 4	1 2 3 4	1 2 3 4	1 2 3 4	I am now interested in learning more.
1 2 3 4	1 2 3 4	1 2 3 4	1 2 3 4	I will act on the material in my organization.
1 2 3 4	1 2 3 4	1 2 3 4	1 2 3 4	The multimedia presented was relevant.

Presentation Delivery:

1 2 3 4	1 2 3 4	1 2 3 4	1 2 3 4	Presenter was prepared and persuasive.
1 2 3 4	1 2 3 4	1 2 3 4	1 2 3 4	Presenter has a strong grasp on the subject.
1 2 3 4	1 2 3 4	1 2 3 4	1 2 3 4	Presentation style was compelling.
1 2 3 4	1 2 3 4	1 2 3 4	1 2 3 4	Visuals were legible and relevant.

The Standard Response Protocol:

1 2 3 4	The SRP is practical for my situation.
1 2 3 4	I have the authority to implement the SRP in my school, district, department or agency.
1 2 3 4	I have the ability to be an advocate for implementing the SRP.
1 2 3 4	I would recommend the SRP to my school, district, department or agency.
1 2 3 4	Some colleagues take an "It Can't Happen Here" position in regard to school violence.

Other:

What were your greatest takeaways from the presentation about the Standard Response Protocol?

_____

_____

If you would like to stay up to date on the I "Love U Guys" Foundation, the Standard Response Protocol, or any of our other initiatives, please feel free to leave us your contact info.

My name: _____

My email: _____

standard™ response protocol

Student Safety

A critical ingredient in the safe school recipe is the classroom response to an incident at school. Weather events, fire, accidents, intruders and other threats to student safety are scenarios that are planned and trained for by students, teachers, staff and administration.

SRP

Our school is expanding the safety program to include the Standard Response Protocol (SRP). The SRP is based on these four actions. Lockout, Lockdown, Evacuate and Shelter. In the event of an emergency, the action and appropriate direction will be called on the PA.

Lockout - "Secure the Perimeter"
Lockdown - "Locks, Lights, Out of Sight"
Evacuate - "To the Announced Location"
Shelter - "Using Announced Type and Method"

Training

Please take a moment to review these actions. Students and staff will be trained and the school will drill these actions over the course of the school year.

More information can be found at http://iloveuguys.org

Lockout
Secure the Perimeter
Lockout is called when there is a threat or hazard outside of the school building.

Students:
- Return to inside of building
- Do business as usual

Teachers
- Recover students and staff from outside building
- Increased situational awareness
- Do business as usual
- Take roll, account for students

Lockdown
Locks, Lights, Out of Sight
Lockdown is called when there is a threat or hazard inside the school building.

Students:
- Move away from sight
- Maintain silence

Teachers:
- Lock classroom door
- Lights out
- Move away from sight
- Maintain silence
- Wait for First Responders to open door
- Take roll, account for students

Evacuate
To the Announced Location
Evacuate is called to move students and staff from one location to another.

Students:
- Leave stuff behind
- Form a single file line
- Take the hands of person in front and behind
- Be prepared for alternatives during response.

Teachers:
- Grab roll sheet if possible
- Lead students to Evacuation Location
- Take roll, account for students

Shelter
Using the Announced Type and Method
Shelter is called when the need for personal protection is necessary.

Types:
- For Tornado
- For Bomb
- For Hazmat

Methods:
- Drop, Cover and Hold
- And Seal
- In Silence

Students:
- Use Appropriate Method

Teachers:
- Use Appropriate Method
- Take roll, account for students

GEAR

Anything new is always considered the devil's tool.

Rip Torn

PRESENTATION GEAR AND STUFF

If you are doing keynotes, plenaries or workshops more than 6 times a year, then you might want to consider getting some gear. You owe your audience your comfort on stage. If there are honorariums or speakers fees, then use these to fund your gear acquisition.

GET A CLICKER IMMEDIATELY. GO! NOW!

At the very bare minimum, get a clicker. Preferably with a bright laser pointer. And test setting it up. Test it on your desktop computer. Test it on your laptop. Test setting it up on your friend's and neighbor's computers. With luck you will never need to set it up on an alien machine, prior to your presentation, but if so, you need to have some familiarity with the process.

You also need it to practice your presentation. The clicker should not be a discovery item on presentation day.

TESTING, ONE, TWO, THREE

Get a handheld microphone. Wireless if possible. It may come in handy for other things, but you need to get your mic technique down. Recording your rehearsals is an important exercise. Both Powerpoint and Keynote let you record as you rehearse. You need to listen to what you say. How you say it. How often "Ummm" gets used. How often you fade away from your mic. How often you get too close. Practice changing its batteries too.

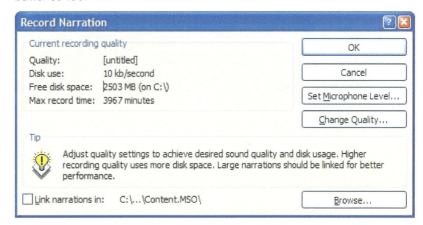

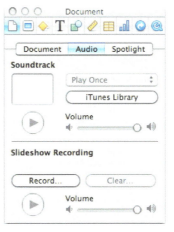

In PowerPoint you can record narration under the Slide Show ribbon. In Keynote, choose the Document Inspector and select the Audio tab

The other benefit of a microphone is quality. Your hand held mic will be of higher quality than the internal mic on your laptop. This means that if you need to create a pre-recorded "talk-through" version of your presentation, you have the ability to provide a higher quality product.

BE A TV STAR

If you don't have one, get a video camera and a tripod. These can be pretty cheap, but you absolutely need to video tape both your practice sessions and your presentations. Worst case, borrow one. These recordings don't need to be super high quality, just enough for review. You must make time to watch them.

If you have a colleague that is at your actual presentation, have them set up the video camera for that as well. (The reason I suggest a colleague is that on presentation day, you need to focus on your audience and your performance. No other distractions or awkwardness.)

ADAPTERS AND CABLES

As your presentations become more media laden, you may make the decision to always bring your own laptop to make the presentation. Even more likely if you use a Mac versus a Windows machine. With that in mind here's a list of adapters and cables I carry.

DVI TO VGA ADAPTER.

 My MacBook Pro has DVI video out. So, I have a couple of these DVI to VGA adapters with me at all times. Why two? I had a multi-stop engagement in New Jersey and New York. When I disconnected the laptop from the gig in Jersey, I forgot to grab the adapter. Meant a little bit of scrambling when I got to New York. Now, I always carry two.

BEHRINGER U-CONTROL UCA202 USB-AUDIO INTERFACE

Some venues are more susceptible to ground loop when you plug your laptop audio into the house sound system. You know, that annoying buzz or hum. This redirects audio via USB and often makes buzz and hum go away.

THREE WAY OUTLET.

Not only handy at the venue, it's handy when traveling. When every outlet is taken by other electricity vampires at the airport terminal, you can share, and maybe even make a new friend with this handy gadget.

LIVE WIRE 1/8" (TRS) - DUAL 1/4" Y CABLE

 I can't tell you how many times this cable has saved my butt. A lot of portable PAs don't have 1/8" stereo inputs. But they almost always have 1/4" mono inputs. This cable is a must have.

You can find this online.[19]

> ""
> Now pay attention, 007. I want you to take great care of this equipment. There are one or two rather special accessories..
> ""
>
> *Q*

> ""
> Q, have I ever let you down?
> ""
>
> *James Bond*

> ""
> Frequently!
> ""
>
> *Q*

FLICKR

Here is the only picture and story I've posted on Flickr. It got over 20,000 hits in three days. Featured on TUAW. (http://tuaw.com) Figured it was time to quit while I was ahead.

If it wasn't for Synergy (synergy2.sourceforge.net), this would be a carpal-tunnel breeding zone. Five Macs, three PCs and a Linux box. All driven by one keyboard and mouse, with seamless screen switching across machines.

Lots of browsers open. Apache Logs. BBEdit. Photoshop. For web development it's 11,600 horizontal pixels of heaven.

BATTERIES

Every decade or so I go to rechargeable batteries. I'm on that track right now. I carry a couple of spares of every type of battery I might need. Including 9 volts (which aren't rechargeable, darn it), for wireless mics. (I've hot swapped mic batteries during a media clip, while presenting.)

GAFFER'S OR DUCT TAPE

Get duct tape. Put it in your bag. Bored? Make a wallet.

IF YOU'RE REALLY SERIOUS, GET A PROJECTOR

Get a projector if you are doing lots of presentations. There is some expense here, but having your own projector may save the day, or provide more presentation opportunities. It also gives you a better rehearsal experience.

If you have audio or video clips in your presentation, then get a pretty good 2.1 computer sound system. Here's what I mean. With a powered subwoofer and strong satellite speakers you can produce a remarkable amount of noise, even in a high school gymnasium. Certainly, more than enough for a conference room.

YOUR STUDIO. YES, I CALLED YOUR OFFICE A STUDIO

The baseline studio is a PC with PowerPoint. You may also need a simple audio editor and a video editor. I used to be able to talk about multimedia applications on the Windows side of the world. Now, I just don't.

But I do suggest that you get Firefox and find and install the Download Helper Plugin. This one lets you download videos from YouTube and other popular video sharing services.

MY STUDIO

I must admit that I'm kind of a zealot geek when it comes to presentations. Actually, computers in general. We live in amazing times. What can be done in a home office is really quite remarkable. I use a Mac for all of my presentation creation. I use Keynote to build my presentations. I also create my own video clips or edit stuff I find online. For video editing I usually use Final Cut Express. For audio I use Logic Express, Soundtrack and SparkLE.

But the foundation is Keynote. I also have to move presentations to PowerPoint for Windows. So I have a Windows PC.

In my past life I wrote software. Mostly web applications. (Sometimes I tell folks that I was doing web 2.0 when version 1 was still in beta.) What that meant was I have a number of machines that I work on simultaneously. Macs. Windows. Linux. Each with its own monitor. I found a cool thing though. "Synergy." Synergy lets me share one keyboard and mouse with all of the machines. What this means is that it looks like one giant desktop, even though it's multiple computers and multiple monitors. Yeah, I know. Zealot Geek.

RANTING

Phase 1: Identify the market leader.

Phase 2: Emulate the market leader.

Phase 3: Steal the vision, provide a migration path.

Phase 4: Integrate, leverage and erode, erode, erode.

Jupiter Communications
Microsoft Internet Strategy Report

Note: I might have gotten a little exuberant on Phase 4. Just one erode once may have been more accurate.

A SHORT RANT ON THE POWERPOINT USER INTERFACE

Some of this stuff shouldn't be hard, but the Redmond minions are a naughty bunch. The interface for PowerPoint for Windows is more than annoying. It seems intentionally cruel. The "Ribbon" interface is the single worst evolutionary step in the history of human/computer interaction.

The constant changing of the idiot ribbon is confusing. Why does the ribbon interface go back to Home after some actions and not others? Any semblance of fine positioning control is buried in dialogs that go away when you hit the return key instead of in palettes. The lack of palettes is a clear indication that the concept of precision is still under development at Microsoft.

And my older version of PowerPoint on the Mac has irritating fades and changes of the palettes that frankly induce illogical rage. Hello! Microsoft! Don't do "Context Sensitive" stuff until you get it right.

" So many PowerPoint slide decks look like they were crafted by **drunken monkeys**."

It's really no wonder so many PowerPoint slide decks look like they were crafted by drunken monkeys. Users simply want to leave the frustration of using PowerPoint as quickly as possible. Now, you might think that I'm some sort of Mac fanboi who is simply doing a little gratuitous Microsoft bashing.

It's actually a little different than that. I developed web-based software for years. So I have several Windows machines, as well as Macs, to test different web browsers and versions.

Currently, I do a lot of presentation development. That demands I package presentations for Windows PowerPoint. Again, spending time in a Windows world. Believe me, it's not without cursing.

ANYMORE, IT'S KEYNOTE

But, I gotta be honest with you. Anymore, I do the heavy lifting of presentation design on a Mac. In Keynote. It's simply faster and more precise to build there, and export to PowerPoint and fix the naughties.

Before you softies jump in to complain, if you haven't used both PowerPoint and Keynote to actually build or tune presentations, you really don't know what you're talking about. If you have, and prefer PowerPoint, more power to you. (If you want, tell me why... email: trolltime@carpeaudience.com. You may have seen this rant coming when you read the subtitle of this book.)

All that said, whether it's PowerPoint or Keynote, I still look at how wonderful the ability to quickly create visual support for a presentation is. Full color images, text, charts, audio and video. Wow. Remember, "People learn more deeply from words and pictures than from words alone." What can be done with a laptop, a cappuccino, and an internet connection at an outdoor cafe, under a green canvas umbrella is simply astounding. Have I mentioned that we live in amazing times?

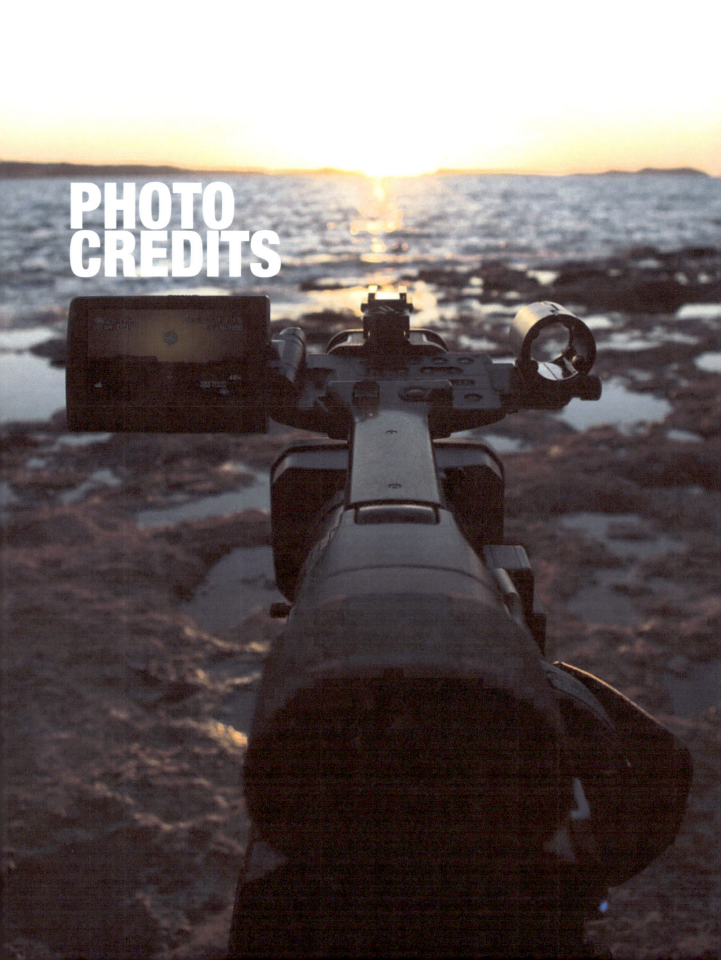

PHOTO
CREDITS

STEVE AND SARA EMRY

http://www.flickr.com/people/emry/

Plus a little twisting in Photoshop

INGRID AT ONE MEANING

http://onemeaning.com

This photograph was taken on Karen Chesleigh's (my business parter) birthday at the Butterfly Conservatory at the Museum of Natural History on March 1, 2011 - we were hoping her mom's spirit would land on her like a butterfly.

LASCAUX CAVE PAINTING

Yes, I know that the paintings predate 2010 b.c. It was just irresistible.

STOCK EXCHANGE

http://www.sxc.hu/photo/1266835

PHOTO BUCKET

http://s127.photobucket.com/home/rosiekisses

"BRAIN SCAN" - MACK SCHROER

http://mschroer.wordpress.com/art-galleries/conceptual-art/

I found this stunning piece while looking a traditional brain scan/cat scan image. I emailed the artist, requesting permission, and within a day got an email back. Please take a moment and look at some of this artist's other work.

LIVE AT THE THUNDERDOME

http://www.zooomr.com/photos/aqui_ali/3129773/

MAX GONZALEZ

Max took this photo in Africa. He said his guide just reached down and suddenly there was a scorpion in hand. Max admitted later that unlike birds, two in the bush are just fine.

STOCK EXCHANGE
http://www.sxc.hu/profile/ctechs

STOCK EXCHANGE
http://www.sxc.hu/profile/JoanaCroft

FRACTALS
http://www.logic.at/staff/gmeiner/JFractals/index.html

OPEN WALLS
http://www.openwalls.com

MY CONFINED SPACE
http://myconfinedspace.com

CLAY MARKWELL
http://thislifefromscratch.blogspot.com/

Here is another example of how "Ask and you shall receive," works. A quick email to Clay. A rapid response with permission to use.

I "heart" the internet.

FLICKR
Gustovo G.

http://www.flickr.com/photos/gustavog/

MORGUEFILE
Photo courtesy of Kenn W. Kiser

http://www.morguefile.com/creative/click

STOCK EXCHANGE
http://www.sxc.hu/profile/Egilshay

Kym McLeod

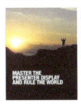

STOCK EXCHANGE
http://www.sxc.hu/profile/winterb6

Bryan Wintersteen

STOCK EXCHANGE
http://www.sxc.hu/profile/iwd

Chris Cummings

VINTAGE PRINTABLE
http://vintageprintable.com/wordpress/

MERPOWER
http://merpower.wordpress.com/2008/08/19/vital-hand-tools-for-your-boat/

STOCK EXCHANGE
http://www.sxc.hu/photo/1266835

STOCK EXCHANGE
http://www.sxc.hu/profile/noguerajef

Jefferson Noguera

FLICKR
Inside the Wild West Store

Photo by Dave Wilson
http://www.flickr.com/photos/dawilson/2793319903/

WHERE'D YOU GET ALL OF THIS STUFF

REFERENCES

[1] The Standard Response Protocol is based not on individual scenarios but on the response to any given scenario. Like the Incident Command System (ICS), SRP demands a specific vocabulary but also allows for great flexibility. The premise is simple - there are four specific actions that can be performed during an incident. When communicating these actions, the action is labeled with a "Term of Art" and is then followed by a "Directive". Execution of the action is performed by active participants, including students, staff, teachers and first responders.

Lockout is followed by the Directive: "Secure the Perimeter" and is the protocol used to safeguard students and staff within the building.

Lockdown is followed by "Locks, Lights, Out of Sight" and is the protocol used to secure individual rooms and keep students quiet and in place.

Evacuate is always followed by a location, and is used to move students and staff from one location to a different location in or out of the building.

Shelter is always followed by a type and a method and is the protocol for group and self protection.

[2] On September 27th, 2006 a gunman entered Platte Canyon High School, held seven girls hostage and ultimately shot and killed Emily Keyes. During the time she was held hostage, Emily sent her parents text messages... "I love you guys" and "I love u guys. k?" Emily's kindness, spirit, fierce joy, and the dignity and grace that followed this tragic event define the core of The "I Love U Guys" Foundation.
http://iloveuguys.org

[3] John Scully relates this story when he was recruited by Steve Jobs to Apple Computer. "And then he looked up at me and just stared at me with the stare that only Steve Jobs has and he said do you want to sell sugar water for the rest of your life or do you want to come with me and change the world and I just gulped because I knew I would wonder for the rest of my life what I would have missed."
http://www.pbs.org/nerds/part3.html

[4] Seth Godin - Really Bad PowerPoint (And How to Avoid it) This was seminal read. I had been minimalizing the visuals of my presentations with some success
http://www.sethgodin.com/freeprize/reallybad-1.pdf

[5] Richard Mayer - Multimedia Learning
Richard E. Mayer is Professor of Psychology at the University of California, Santa Barbara (UCSB) where he has served since 1975. He received a Ph.D. in Psychology from the University of Michigan in 1973, and served as a Visiting Assistant Professor of Psychology at Indiana University from 1973 to 1975. His research interests are in educational and cognitive psychology. His current research involves the intersection of cognition, instruction, and technology with a special focus on multimedia learning and computer-supported learning.
http://www.psych.ucsb.edu/people/faculty/mayer/index.php

[6] Garr Reynolds - Presentation Zen: Simple Ideas on Presentation Design and Delivery.
Recommended reading.
http://www.presentationzen.com/

[7] T.J. Walker - Presentation Training A-Z
Presentation Training A-Z is a compilation of insights from TJ Walker's 20 years of training experience. The book addresses all aspects of public speaking, from learning how to develop a strong opening to creating a powerful closing and even understanding how to execute it.

[8] Effective Business Communication and Barriers
http://www.slideshare.net/carol_sim/effective-business-communication-barriers

[9] Richard Mayer - Multimedia Learning

[10] John Medina - Brain Rules
Medina is an affiliate Professor of Bioengineering at the University of Washington School of Medicine. He is also the director of the Brain Center for Applied Learning Research at Seattle Pacific University. Medina lives in Seattle, Washington, with his wife and two boys.
http://www.brainrules.net/

[11] John Medina - Brain Rules

[12] The Standard Response Protocol

[13] Garr Reynolds - Presentation Zen

[14] Matt Davis on word recognition.
http://www.mrc-cbu.cam.ac.uk/people/matt.davis/cmabridge/index.html

[15] Seth Godin's Three Laws of Great Graphs
http://sethgodin.typepad.com/seths_blog/2008/07/the-three-laws.html

[16] Brent Dykes is the PowerPoint Ninja. Whether or not I agree with everything he says, his blog is a great read and a great resource. And if it turns out that you really do need a sexy curvy animated arrow, this is the place to go to learn how.
http://www.powerpointninja.com

[17] Lt. Col. Dave Grossman is an internationally recognized scholar, author, soldier, and speaker who is one of the world's foremost experts in the field of human aggression and the roots of violence and violent crime.
http://www.killology.com/

[18] Edward Tufte - The Cognitive Style Of Powerpoint: Pitching Out Corrupts Within
http://www.edwardtufte.com/bboard/q-and-a-fetch-msg?msg_id=0001yB&topic_id=1

[19] Musician's Friend
http://backstage.musiciansfriend.com/Accessories/Cables-Snakes/Audio--RCA-Cables/1-8-TRS--Dual-1-4-Y-Cable-10-Foot.site1sku330481000000154.sku

www.ingramcontent.com/pod-product-compliance
Lightning Source LLC
LaVergne TN
LVHW071522070326
832902LV00002B/40